THE TWINKIE SQUAD

Other Books by GORDON KORMAN:

Losing Joe's Place
Radio Fifth Grade
The Zucchini Warriors
A Semester in the Life of a Garbage Bag
Son of Interflux
Don't Care High
Our Man Weston
No Coins, Please
Who Is Bugs Potter?
Bugs Potter LIVE at Nicaninny
I Want to Go Home!
The War with Mr. Wizzle
Go Jump in the Pool!
Beware the Fish!
This Can't Be Happening at Macdonald Hall!
Macdonald Hall Goes Hollywood

By GORDON KORMAN and BERNICE KORMAN:

The D– Poems of Jeremy Bloom:
  A Collection of Poems About School,
  Homework, and Life (sort of)

GORDON KORMAN
THE
TWINKIE
SQUAD

**SCHOLASTIC
HARDCOVER**

Scholastic Inc.
New York

Library of Congress Cataloging-in-Publication Data

Korman, Gordon.
     The Twinkie Squad / by Gordon Korman.
        p.   cm.
     Summary: Chaos spreads when Douglas, the most eccentric sixth-grader
in Thaddeus G. Little Middle School, joins the Twinkie Squad, a special
counseling group for problem students.
                        ISBN 0-590-45249-5
     [1. Schools — Fiction.   2. Humorous stories.]   I. Title.
PZ7.K8369Tw   1992
[Fic] — dc20   91-30382
                                                             CIP
                                                              AC

12 11 10 9 8 7 6 5 4   4 5 6 7/9

                        Printed in the U.S.A.   37

                First Scholastic printing, October 1992

For Annie Dorobis,
The Washingtonian

Contents

THE TWINKIE SQUAD

1

A Blob
of Something
Different

The morning recess at Thaddeus G. Little Middle School was in full swing when the limousine arrived. It was long and silver, the stretch kind. As it whispered up to the curb at the school's front entrance, jump ropes fell idle, tape players were switched off, and basketball rebounds dropped to the ancient pavement of the playground. Recess spilled out of the yard to surround the limo.

A slim, stylishly dressed woman emerged from the backseat of the car and stood for a moment, scanning the crowd of curious sixth-, seventh-, and eighth-graders. Her eyes fell on the only one of them not mobbing her car, a very tall, blond sixth-grader seated on the front steps. She waved, but he was making notes in a bright yellow ring binder propped against his knees, and did not seem to notice.

"Fight!"

The cry came from the back of the throng. At the

center of the group, a shoving match broke out, and the mob began to sway and ripple like a giant swamp creature. Soon it boiled back into the schoolyard, along with the chant: *"Fight! . . . Fight! . . . Fight!"*

Even a stretch limo could not interrupt recess for more than a few minutes.

The woman stared after them in perplexity, then turned to the boy who still sat on the front steps.

"Well, Douglas? Are you going to say hello, or are you embarrassed to have a mother in front of your friends?"

Douglas stood up in a tangle of long legs. "Of course not," he said mildly. "What would I be doing with friends?" He snapped his binder firmly shut and approached his mother. "How was Rome? I thought you weren't coming home till tonight."

"Your father stayed at the Summit. I took the early plane because my secretary said your principal called five times. Douglas, is there anything you want to tell me before I go in there?"

"Mr. Silverman probably just wants to meet you," said her son airily. "Everybody knows you give the most famous parties in Washington. Maybe he's trying to get on the guest list."

"Douglas, this is the public school system. It's not like all those private schools you were kicked out of. If you don't fit in here, there's no place left to send you. We'd have to move to another city. And your father might have trouble finding work as a U.S. ambassador in Omaha!" Grasping his arm, she propelled the two of them through the heavy metal front doors. As they disappeared inside the school, they could still hear the shouts from the playground:

"Fight! . . . Fight! . . . Fight!"

"I don't know how you manage to get into so much trouble," she went on. "No one can even tell me what it is you do — just that they can't stand it, and they won't put up with it."

Douglas drew himself up to his full height, which, for a sixth-grader, was an amazing five feet eleven inches. "Schools are just like factories. You put a blob of plastic into the machine, and it spits out a little toy triceratops. Everything is fine as long as all the triceratopses are exactly alike. But when a blob of something different comes along, they've got to get rid of it before the whole machine breaks down."

She looked at him. "What if the blob of something different loses his allowance for a month?"

Douglas shrugged. "Money is totally irrelevant to my life style."

"Douglas, your attitude — " She was on the verge of a display of temper when the school secretary spied her and emitted a cry of delight.

"Mrs. Fairchild!" she gushed, rushing over. "What an honor! You look just like your pictures in the society pages!"

"How do you do," Mrs. Fairchild responded graciously. "I have an appointment to see Mr. Silverman."

"Yes, yes, of course!" Completely star-struck, the secretary made no move to buzz the inner office. "Is it true that the Vice President and the French ambassador played a duet from *Oklahoma* on the piano at your last party?"

Mrs. Fairchild laughed politely. "You can't believe everything you read."

The door to the inner office burst open, and out

strode Mr. Silverman. He was a young man who looked more like a high school senior than a principal. Very much aware of this, he did everything he could to appear older. He had grown a giant bushy mustache. A scraggly beard almost, but not quite, concealed rosy apple cheeks.

"Thank you for coming, Mrs. Fairchild," he greeted her. "And may I say what an honor it is that you and the ambassador chose our school for Douglas. I'm sure you'll find this is just the atmosphere you've been looking for."

At that moment, a beefy eighth-grader roared into the office, holding a bloody handkerchief to his nose, and wailing at the top of his lungs.

The principal stared in horror. "Michael, what happened? Who did this to you?"

"Commando!" the boy howled. "Commando did it! It was Commando!"

Mr. Silverman looked bewildered. "Commando?! What commando? Where?"

As if on cue, a teacher marched in, leading a small skinny dark boy with blazing eyes. His jet-black hair was short on top and stood up in spikes, but hung long and straight everywhere else, brushing his shoulders. From his left ear, a silver coiled cobra dangled. His nose was bloodier than Michael's, but not a word of complaint came from him.

Mr. Silverman took one look at him and groaned. "Oh. Armando. Again."

Commando pointed at Mrs. Fairchild. "Hey, cool! Ambassador Fairchild's wife!" He frowned. "Why aren't you in Rome at the Summit?"

Mrs. Fairchild just stared.

* * *

MEMO

TO: D.C. Northeast School Bus
        Company

FROM: Douglas Fairchild, Esq.
        passenger

Gentlemen:
   I have been riding your bus now for three weeks, and wish to draw the following to your attention:
   1) Your service is not prompt. Three times in the past week I have been forced to wait at least two minutes in inclement weather. As my attached medical records will confirm, I am subject to postnasal drip, which is aggravated by damp and cold.
   2) Your vehicle is unsafe. On a sharp turn on G Street Northeast yesterday, I could feel the bus very nearly tipping over. When I attempted to organize my fellow passengers to lean to the left to maintain balance, the driver became abusive.
   3) Your employee, the driver, is woefully lacking in concentration. On my first ride with her, I attempted a routine test, which involved bouncing raisins intermittently off the back of her head. She lost concentration, pulled the bus to the curb without checking her mirrors or signaling, and commenced an assault on my person.
   Accordingly, I will now be traveling to

school exclusively by taxi. Please let me know if you wish the taxi company to bill you directly, or if you would prefer that I pay my own fare and invoice you on a monthly basis.

Yours, etc.,

Douglas Fairchild

Mrs. Fairchild put down the letter. "I'm very sorry, Mr. Silverman but, as you can see, I'm not surprised."

The principal gawked. "He does this often?"

She smiled briefly. "The ambassador and I have three children. Our older son is a congressman, our daughter is a world-renowned research physician, and then there's Douglas. It hasn't been easy for Douglas, having a famous father and two successful adult siblings. When he was four years old, he tried to fire his nanny for unfair cookie rationing. And he's been at it ever since."

Mr. Silverman glanced at the file in front of him. "Four private schools in two years," he commented.

"The public system seems like our only answer." She glanced out the window in the office door. Beside Douglas sat Commando, bleeding and awaiting his turn with the principal.

"Don't worry, Mrs. Fairchild," said Mr. Silverman confidently. "I think we have just the program for Douglas. Mr. and Mrs. Richardson, our guidance counsellors, run an afternoon group session for boys and girls who take a little longer to settle in.

"Well, if you say so." She looked dubious. "But

you *will* keep an eye on him? Douglas is different, even for someone who's different."

"Pssst — yo, Doug."

On the bench outside the principal's office, Douglas glanced up from his yellow binder and slanted a look down at Commando.

"Are you really Ambassador Fairchild's kid?"

Douglas nodded and returned to his writing.

"Man, you guys are high society! What are you doing in this dump?"

Douglas looked impatient. "I was given my choice of schools, and this is the one I selected."

"Man, it must be amazing — seeing your folks on TV, getting to meet famous people! What's it like to have the President over for dinner?"

"Pretty good," said Douglas, "so long as he doesn't hog the potatoes. And he has to promise to keep down the noise. I'm writing a book."

Commando tapped at his nose to see if it was still bleeding. It was. In addition, his lips were beginning to swell. "What kind of book?"

"A complete history of Pefkakia."

"Pef-*what*?"

Douglas was offended. "Pefkakia. It's a small west-Asian nation, and it happens to be my native country."

Commando frowned. "What native country? You're from the most American family in town!"

"Oh, my parents and my brother and sister are all Americans. I'm the only Pefkakian."

"Come on! If your folks are American, so are you."

"I'm American, too," Douglas admitted. "But since I was actually born on Pefkakian soil, I have dual citizenship." From his pocket he produced a tattered photocopy of an unusual-looking document written in English, French, and a strange language that looked like a cross between ancient Egyptian and chicken footprints. The English part attested to the fact that, on October 13, 1981, in Pefkakia City, Pefkakia, a man child, Douglas Herbert Fairchild, was born.

Commando was impressed. "But you're more American, right?"

"Absolutely not," said Douglas. "As soon as I turn eighteen, I intend to move back."

"It's that good, huh? I never heard of it."

Douglas smiled tolerantly. "We Pefkakians like it that way. We want to keep our country simple and happy, just as it was in the days of the immortal Ano Pefki." Ano Pefki was the founder and first prime minister of Pefkakia. Douglas was just about one hundred percent completely, totally sure (almost) that Pefki was a great leader.

"Washington's happy," said Commando defensively.

"Too hectic," replied Douglas, returning his attention to his binder. "Now, if you'll excuse me — " He began writing in his notebook.

"That's your book?" Commando reached out eagerly. "Let me see."

With a cry of outrage, Douglas slammed the binder shut, and hugged it to his chest. A loud sound, somewhere between a snort and a honk, erupted from his nose.

Commando was horrified. "Are you okay?"

"You've aggravated my postnasal drip!" Douglas accused.

Sympathetically, Commando held out his blood-stained, filthy handkerchief.

Douglas ignored the gesture and began trying to clear his throat.

The school nurse, Mrs. Chung, bustled into the office. "Okay, Armando," she said with a tired smile. "Michael's going to live, no thanks to you. What's your damage report this time? Everything attached?"

Commando grinned sheepishly. "I just need to wash my face."

"What you *need*," she said, removing the handkerchief and looking at Commando's nose, "is to stop picking fights with gorillas two years older than you and three times your size. Why can't you go at it with a little kid for a change?"

Commando looked stubborn. "Then I'd be no better than Michael."

"Aha!" She was triumphant. "You admit it! You attacked him because he was bullying a smaller boy!"

Commando folded his arms in front of him, just in time for a droplet of blood to splatter on the turned-up cuff of his jean jacket.

"Come on," coaxed Mrs. Chung. "You've already been suspended for fighting. If you have a good reason for this, you tell Mr. Silverman."

"I'm no squealer."

The nurse was exasperated. "Who are you protecting? The guy beats up on kids who can't defend themselves! What could be lower than that?"

"A squealer," said Commando tersely.

"You're impossible!" Mrs. Chung looked half disgusted and half proud. She paused to regard Douglas, who was still clearing his throat.

"He has a postnasal drip," Commando supplied.

"Well, he sounds like a car with a broken muffler."

At that moment, Mr. Silverman opened his door and ushered Mrs. Fairchild into the outer office.

"Good news." Mr. Silverman beamed at Douglas. "You're going to join our Special Discussion Group every day at three-thirty."

There was a gasp from Commando. "That's the Twinkie Squad!"

"Armando," said the principal warningly, "this is none of your business. Go into my office."

"Don't do it, Doug!" Commando hissed.

"That's *enough*!" barked the principal. He turned a smiling face to his visitor. "Thank you for coming, Mrs. Fairchild."

Douglas' mother still looked doubtful. "Please keep me posted on his progress." She regarded her son. "I'm leaving now, Douglas. But we're going to have a discussion about this later when you come home *on the school bus.*"

2

People
Who Think
They're Trees

The cafeteria line was long, and getting longer,
and the standees were becoming rowdy.

"Hey, what's the holdup?"

"Move it along! I'm starving!"

Douglas stood blocking the entire doorway, digging through the cutlery bin, rejecting fork after fork.

"Detergent spots . . . food . . . fingerprints —
disgusting!"

The boy behind him was livid. "What are you,
crazy, kid? Hurry up!"

Douglas was unperturbed. "I have the right not to
eat my lunch with a contaminated piece of silver-
ware. Ah, here we are. A little bent, perhaps, but
clean. And now for a knife."

A loud groan was passed along the line, which
now stretched out into the hall.

Waldo Turcott craned his neck to regard Douglas.
"Who *is* that guy? What's his problem?"

Commando followed his friend's pointing finger. "That's the kid I was telling you about. You know who his dad is? Anton Fairchild."

"Wasn't he the first-round draft pick of the L.A. Lakers?" Waldo was the starting center on Thaddeus G. Little's basketball team, the Minutemen. No other subject ever captured his interest.

"No!" exclaimed Commando impatiently. "Anton Fairchild, the United States ambassador-at-large, one of our top diplomats."

"He's pretty tall for a sixth-grader," commented Waldo thoughtfully. "Does he play?"

The lady behind the counter was pleading with Douglas. "Come on, kid. What do you want to eat?"

"First I would like to see the chef, please," Douglas announced.

"Aw, you saw him yesterday! He's the same guy!"

"He was badly in need of a haircut," Douglas insisted. "I thought I detected a hair in my soup."

"That's gross!" piped a girl having her lunch at a front table. "I'm trying to eat here!"

"Look, we've got meat loaf, mashed potatoes, and peas. Take it or leave it."

Douglas reached for his plate. "Wait a minute. There's something green in here."

About a dozen students pushed their meals away, appetites gone.

"There's nothing green," snapped the server. "It's meat loaf. It's brown."

"Green," he repeated. "Kelly green. Right there." With his pen, he pointed at the main course.

The server reached into her pocket, whipped out a pair of reading glasses, and squinted into the plate. "That's a little piece of onion!"

"Oh, well, that's fine," said Douglas, mollified. "Of course, I can't accept this portion now that you've breathed on it."

Seething, she piled up a new plate, and Douglas moved on to the cash register. There was applause.

With Douglas gone at last, Waldo and Commando moved quickly through the line and emerged into the dining area, carrying their trays. Immediately, Waldo sat down beside Douglas.

"Hey, kid, this is your lucky day. You're going to be backup center for the Thaddeus G. Little Minutemen!"

Douglas stared through him blankly. "Have we been introduced?"

"Hey, Doug." Commando threw a leg over the bench, and took his place at the long cafeteria table. "Meet Waldo. Waldo — Doug."

Waldo offered up a high-five, which Douglas just stared at.

"I know what's scaring you," said Waldo comfortingly. "You think because you're a sixth-grader, you can't cut it on the varsity. But look at Commando here. He's your age, but he's got speed, court sense, and a sweet move to the hoop."

Commando looked up from his meat loaf at Douglas' puzzled expression. "You don't play basketball, do you, Doug?"

"In Pefkakia, our national sport is the medieval biathlon," said Douglas, inventing rapidly. He hadn't been in Pefkakia for a long time, and actually knew very little about the place. Fortunately, neither did anyone else.

"Medieval biathlon!?" Waldo repeated. "What's that?"

"Archery and ring toss." Well, it was *possible*.

Waldo took a long drink of his milk. "You'll get the hang of it. Watch the game on TV tonight, and pay special attention to the centers."

Commando frowned. "What game? All the colleges and pro teams are off tonight."

"Yeah, but Channel Q is showing the Division 3 Junior Yugoslavian All-Stars against the best high school squad in Wyoming."

Commando was half amused and half disgusted. "Who cares? Unless you're from Yugoslavia, or maybe Wyoming."

"I do," said Waldo proudly. "You have no right to call yourself a true basketball fan." He turned back to Douglas. "So, what do you say? Watch the game, and tomorrow we'll have a light workout."

"I have a previous engagement," said Douglas with dignity.

"But you're *tall*! In a couple of years, you'll be eating guys up in the low post!"

"I'm sorry. I've been invited to join the Special Discussion Group."

Waldo's eyes bulged. "The Twinkie Squad?"

Douglas nodded. "It's a social club. Very prestigious."

"I've been meaning to tell you about that," said Commando seriously. "The Twinkie Squad's not a club, Doug. It's more like an insane asylum for students. Not that you're nuts — "

"Thank you," Douglas acknowledged gravely.

"You've got to get out of it," Commando persisted. "I mean, Ambassador Fairchild's kid can't be a Twinkie! It's — it's bad for national security!"

"And you'd miss basketball practice," added Waldo.

"You'd hate it on the Twinkie Squad," Commando went on. "It's all weirdos and space cadets. You know — bed wetters, and people who think they're trees!"

"It's obviously a big mistake," Waldo decided. "A *player* can't be on the Twinkie Squad." He jammed the remainder of his meat loaf and mashed potatoes into his mouth, gulped it down, and stood up. "I'm going to shoot some hoops till next period. Who's with me?" He looked pointedly at Douglas, then broke into a broad grin as Douglas pushed his tray away. But his face fell as he watched his backup center reach for his yellow binder and open it.

"He's writing a book," Commando supplied.

"About what?" asked Waldo dubiously.

"Not about basketball!" Commando stood up. "I'll shoot around for a while." He turned to Douglas. "Think it over, okay? Trust me. You don't want to be a Twinkie."

"Mmmm," murmured Douglas absently. He was already absorbed in his note making.

Douglas stepped into the guidance office and looked around. Empty. He could hear voices coming from a connected conference room. Stealthily, like James Bond, he flattened himself against the wall and peered through the doorway.

The Special Discussion Group was seated around a small oval table. Mr. and Mrs. Richardson were the guidance counsellors in charge. They were a young attractive husband-and-wife team who smiled one hundred percent of the time.

"Today I'd like to talk about feelings," Julia Richardson was saying. "Sometimes we hide our feelings from other people. Do you think this is a good idea?"

The silence that followed was punctuated by a snort of disgust. Julia's smile didn't waver. "Dave? You have a comment?"

Dave Dunn, a paunchy seventh-grader with jet-black hair and a single hedge-thick eyebrow that stretched straight across his forehead, made a sour face. "Feelings stink," he declared. "This school stinks. Washington stinks."

"Honesty," smiled Martin Richardson. "Very good. Now, can you explain *why* it stinks?"

"It just does."

"I agree," said Anita Ditmar with conviction.

"Do you really feel that way?" asked Mrs. Richardson.

Anita hesitated, blue eyes anxious. "Do *you*?" she asked the teacher.

"Of course not! I think life is wonderful!"

"Oh, so do I!" the sixth-grade girl agreed quickly.

Mr. Richardson turned to the boy who was fidgeting directly across from him. "What about you, Ric? What's your opinion of feelings?"

"There's a guy out there," said eighth-grader Ric Ewchuk, jiggling a knee until the room seemed to shake.

"Pardon?"

Ric pointed at the doorway. "There. A guy."

Douglas took a long stride into the conference room. "How do you do?" he said formally. "I'm Douglas Fairchild. Thank you for inviting me."

"You've got the wrong room, kid," growled Dave. "You don't get invited here; you get shafted."

"Welcome, Douglas," beamed Mr. Richardson. "Take a seat. This is an open rap session. You can say anything that's on your mind — "

"Can I say that this group stinks?" came a voice from behind him.

"Quiet, Dave," said Mrs. Richardson.

"I have an attitude problem," Dave informed Douglas confidentially.

"That's quite all right," said Douglas with kind sympathy. "I have a postnasal drip."

"We want you to think of us not as teachers, but as friends," Mr. Richardson told Douglas. "Don't feel you have to call us Mr. and Mrs. Richardson. We are Julia and Martin — right, everybody?"

"Oh, yes, Mr. Richardson," agreed Anita.

The counselor's response was interrupted by the arrival of a tall eighth-grade girl dressed in a long skirt, fringed shawl, and cowboy boots. "Sorry I'm late, boss," she said in a deep voice, and sat down.

Martin gave her a dazzling smile. "Yolanda, you missed four classes again today."

"Hey, pal, I was busy."

Julia smiled with understanding. "Did you go to another movie?"

"Listen, sweet-cakes, I seen guys pumped fulla lead for asking nosy questions!"

Martin snapped his fingers. "The gangster picture over at the Bijou!"

Yolanda nodded. *"Bullets Bitterman Meets Al Capone.* A classic."

Martin sighed, which he managed to do without reducing his smile one notch. "You have to go to your classes, Yolanda."

"What for?" snarled Dave. "They all stink."

"Well, how about you, Gerald?" ventured Mr. Richardson. "We're talking about feelings."

All eyes turned to the youngster sitting scrunched down in his chair. At age ten, Gerald Dooley was the youngest of the group. He was a sixth-grader jumped up from fifth grade. Straight A's did not help the fact that middle school absolutely terrified him. He was studying his feet so intently that only the top of his curly head showed.

"Gerald?" Julia prompted with a gentle smile. "Do you have something to contribute?"

"No." It was barely a whisper.

An uncomfortable silence followed, but nothing could wipe the smiles from the Richardsons' faces.

"Okay," said Martin briskly. "Now's the perfect time to get to know our newcomer. Douglas, is there anything you would like to talk about?"

"Certainly." Douglas leaned forward. "I would like to talk about Pefkakia."

All at once, the Richardsons' twin smiles disappeared.

The bus driver was, as usual, not too friendly. "Well, what do you know — my favorite letter writer. Heard from the bus company yet?"

Douglas took the seat behind the driver. "My only concern is my safety and that of my fellow passengers."

The bus pulled out of the driveway.

"That's a red light," Douglas called.

"Thanks, kid. Without you, I never would have figured it out."

"You're welcome," said Douglas blandly. The light

turned green, and the traffic moved out again.
"Okay, you can speed up now. And watch out for
this guy in the convertible."

The driver laughed. "Real cute. Now, would you
let me drive?"

Douglas pointed to the sign directly over the wind-
shield: PASSENGERS ARE ASKED TO ASSIST THE DRIVER
IN ANY WAY POSSIBLE. "That's what it says, and that's
what I'm doing. We have to yield here."

"I *know* that," said the driver, not quite so
patiently.

"Don't tailgate the cement mixer," Douglas advised. "Every year there are hundreds of cases of
vehicles buried in concrete."

Angrily, the driver pulled out her license and held
it out behind her, in Douglas' face. "You know what
this is, kid?"

Douglas studied it, frowning. "The picture looks
nothing like you," he commented. "Do you have any
other identification? A credit card, perhaps?"

The license snapped out of view. "That's it!"
seethed the driver. "You sit there, and keep your big
mouth shut!"

"Look out!" Douglas bellowed, right in her ear.

Shocked, she slammed on the brakes. The bus
screeched to a halt, jostling students all the way to
the back row. She wheeled in her seat, eyes blazing.
"Are you crazy? What was that for?"

"That was my fault," Douglas admitted graciously.
"I thought that ice-cream truck was an ambulance."

Horns were honking behind them, so the driver
put the bus back in gear. "Kid, if you don't shut your
yap, you're walking the rest of the way!"

Douglas pointed forward. *"Look out!"*

The driver was livid. "If you think I'm going to fall for the same — "

Crash!

The school bus plowed into the rear end of a black limousine with diplomatic plates. The rear door opened, and out stepped Ambassador Anton Fairchild, home at last from the Rome Summit.

The spaghetti sauce simmered on the stove. Commando stood there, a towel tucked under his belt, stirring his concoction with a wooden spoon. He took a taste, nodded his satisfaction, and adjourned to the living room. He slumped in the worn armchair, switching back and forth between videos on MTV and *Political Diary* on PBS.

In the kitchen, a furtive face appeared at the window. Someone was squatting on the fire escape, peering inside. A hand raised the sash slowly and silently, and a dark-haired man in his mid-thirties climbed over the sill. Careful not to make a sound, he dipped a spoon into the spaghetti sauce and brought it to his lips. Savoring thoughtfully, he added a dash of garlic powder.

There was movement in the living room, and the man stiffened like a pointer. He stashed the pot in the cupboard, and flattened himself against the wall, peeking over his shoulder at the kitchen door.

Commando entered and stopped short, gawking at the stove. "Hey, what happened to my — "

The intruder leaped out in front of him, arms and legs spread, and bellowed, *"BOO!"*

Commando jumped back, then relaxed and looked disgusted. "Aw, come on, Dad, act your age."

"I'm acting my mental age," Mr. Rivera said, pleased. "Besides, I had to come in the window. Three times this week you've booby-trapped the front door. What have you got there now — a bucket of Gatorade?"

Commando shrugged. "Just a water balloon. I've got an excuse. I'm eleven; you're thirty-five."

"Thirty-four and a half," amended his father, retrieving the sauce and putting it back on the burner. "Don't rush me." He regarded his son's face critically. "Hey, where'd you get the fat lip? Have you been fighting again?"

Commando shrugged. "I popped a guy. He had it coming."

"Big kid picking on a little kid?"

Commando nodded.

Sighing, Mr. Rivera put a pot of water on to boil. "Aw, Comm, how many times do I have to tell you? *You're* a little kid! Someday one of those big bruisers you fight with is going to put you in the hospital!"

"I can look after myself," said Commando stubbornly.

"Yeah, well, what am I supposed to tell Mr. Silverman?"

Commando grinned. "Do you really want to hear my suggestion?"

"No." Mr. Rivera took out a box of rigatoni and peered into the pot. "Hurry up!" he urged the water. "I've got to get to class early tonight. I'm failing auditing, and there's a guy who's going to let me photocopy his notes."

Commando looked sympathetic. "Don't worry, Dad. When the exams come up, you'll do great."

"The teacher is such a jerk," Mr. Rivera continued.

"He knows this stuff so well that he has no idea what it's like to not understand something. You ask a question, and he looks at you like you're from Mars."

"I'm the one who complains about school, remember?" said Commando, standing on tiptoe to peer into the cupboard. "Real plates, or paper?"

"Up to you. You're doing the dishes."

"Paper it is."

Soon Mr. Rivera was piling two plates with rigatoni and meat sauce. Father and son sat down to dinner.

"So, did you write your mom today?"

Commando dumped grated cheese liberally on his dinner. "Aw, Dad, I never know what to put."

"We got separated, but she's still your mom. Think of something."

Commando smirked. "Maybe I should tell her about all the fights I've been getting into lately."

His father stabbed at his dinner. "Don't tell her that! I had enough trouble explaining your haircut and your earring when she got your school picture."

Commando chewed thoughtfully, then asked the question that had been on his mind all day. "Dad, have you ever heard of Pefkakia?"

Mr. Rivera scratched his head. "I think so. It's one of those tiny little countries way, way out there. Are you doing it in geography?"

Commando shook his head. "There's this kid at school who's a Pefkakian. You'll never guess who his dad is — Anton Fairchild!"

Mr. Rivera was surprised. "I thought all those political types sent their kids to private schools."

"Not Doug," said Commando. "You should see this guy, Dad. He's taller than you are, and he talks real weird, like an English professor."

His father smiled. "He's putting you on, Comm. Why would Ambassador Fairchild's son be a foreigner?"

"He's American, too, but he's really into being from Pefkakia," Commando explained. "I saw his birth certificate."

Mr. Rivera raised an eyebrow. "It's possible, you know. These diplomats are all over the world. If your friend was born in Pefkakia, he probably has dual citizenship, and he's making a big deal out of it, just to be different."

Commando grinned oddly. "Doug doesn't have to be foreign to be different."

Mr. Rivera checked his watch, pushed his plate away, and stood up. "I'm out of here. I'll be back around ten." He headed for the front door, disarmed the water balloon, and was gone, tossing over his shoulder, "Write your mother."

"Yeah, yeah, yeah."

"Five minutes back in Washington! Five minutes!" Ambassador Anton Fairchild was marching back and forth in the spacious living room of his penthouse. "I've been greeted in a lot of ways — brass bands, prime ministers, rock-throwing protesters — but never before has anybody deliberately directed a bus into the back of my car!"

Douglas looked sublimely innocent. "I cannot be held responsible for someone else's nervous reaction. I didn't do anything."

The ambassador grimaced. "You *never* do anything, and still trouble manages to follow you around like a tail! I shudder to think what would happen if you actually *did* something! The mind boggles!"

"You're tired," said Douglas tolerantly. "It's jet lag."

"It's whiplash!" his father snapped back. "Have you ever been rear-ended by a seven-ton bus?"

"Well, it was a jolt for me, too," Douglas explained reasonably. "I suffered a relapse of my postnasal drip." He snorted for emphasis.

The ambassador turned to his wife. "Does he really have a postnasal drip?"

Mrs. Fairchild shrugged helplessly. "The doctor says he has a few minor nasal allergies."

"Minor?!" squawked Douglas in outrage.

"This house is always enveloped in mist from the vaporizers and humidifiers," the ambassador complained. "The last time we had the President over, his glasses kept fogging up! It's embarrassing!"

"Well, pardon me for wanting to breathe!"

At bedtime, though, the first thing Douglas did was turn off the cold-steam vaporizer in his room. It made all his clothes clammy.

Douglas had a whole wing of the huge penthouse, which gave him his own living room, a large bedroom, and a private bath. In all that space, the only decoration was the original of his Pefkakian birth certificate. Elaborately framed, it held the place of honor above Douglas' bed. When he was younger, he had plastered his suite with a blinding collage of press clippings about his father the ambassador, his mother the society queen, his brother the congressman, and his sister the genius.

He lay down on the bed. In Pefkakia, he was pretty sure, success was measured in simpler ways. Yes, Anton Fairchild was famous and respected and important. But did he have the freedom to frolic amidst the bullrushes? Douglas hadn't been to Pefkakia in

a long time, but he was almost positive that all Pefkakians frolicked. It was the bullrushes he wasn't
quite so clear about. Surely there were lakes and
rivers? But if Pefkakia was a desert country, they
could frolic amidst the sand dunes. Or if there were
mountains, they could frolic amidst the snowcapped
peaks. That was all okay with Douglas. The important thing was the freedom to frolic.

3

A Bad Hop

" . . . With liberty and justice for all."

The Pledge of Allegiance had ended for all the students but one. As everybody else sat down, Douglas towered over his desk, hand on his heart.

"And I further pledge allegiance to Pefkakia, the land of my birth." He took his seat, amid snickers.

"Rivera — for three! Swish!"

It was morning recess, and Commando and Waldo were at their usual schoolyard court, shooting baskets and drilling one-on-one. With them was Beverly Busby, head cheerleader, student council president, and easily the most popular girl in the school.

Beverly caught the ball and tossed it to Waldo, calling, "Dunk it!"

"Forget it!" laughed Commando.

But the center had already started his approach.

He took three mammoth strides, and launched himself up at the basket. He was six inches too low. The ball slammed into the side of the rim and bounced off into the playground, scattering a game of jump rope. Still laughing, Commando jogged after it.

"I've done it," Waldo told Beverly. "Man, when nobody's watching, I do it all the time!" Suddenly, he pointed across the schoolyard. "Hey, it's my backup center!" He began waving at Douglas, who was seated on a curbstone, writing in his binder.

Beverly stared in horror. "That guy's on the *Twinkie Squad*!"

Everybody always knew who was in the Special Discussion Group because the conference room had one glass wall to the front hall, the busiest part of the building.

"It's some kind of mix-up," shrugged Waldo. "Look at him. He's a natural."

"I don't like it," said Beverly. "If a Twinkie made the Minutemen, I'd quit the cheerleaders like *that*!" She snapped her fingers.

"Hey, Doug!" Commando had also noticed Douglas. He began dribbling the ball. "Here's Rivera — what quickness! Now he sees Fairchild open, and makes a beautiful bounce-pass!"

The ball took a bad hop, and ricocheted upwards. It caught Douglas square on the nose. At first he just sat there, looking shocked. A split second later, blood was pouring out of his nose, down his chin, and all over his shirt.

Commando ran up to him. "Doug! You okay? Why didn't you catch it?"

Douglas' voice was nasal and muffled. "My hands were full." He held up his binder.

"Well, you could've dropped it!"

"My history of Pefkakia?" Douglas was outraged. "Never!"

Commando produced a wadded-up tissue and tried to clean off Douglas' face. "You sure are a bleeder, man. You look like your throat's cut."

"My nose is very sensitive," bubbled Douglas. "This isn't going to do my postnasal drip any good."

Just then, Mr. Silverman came rushing onto the scene. "Douglas! Are you all right?"

"Oh, yeah, no problem," laughed Commando. "He just — "

The principal cast him a murderous glare. "I'll see you in my office."

Commando was taken aback. "But I didn't do anything — "

"And ask Nurse Chung to come out here!" Mr. Silverman interrupted.

"Just a nurse?" mused Douglas dubiously. "Do you happen to have a good allergist? There's a post-nasal drip involved."

"*Now*, Armando!" barked the principal.

Commando waited patiently as Mr. Silverman rif-fled through the folder. When he put the file down, the principal's round face was very grim.

"You have always been aggressive, even in ele-mentary school. Your record says you fought two third-graders — *in kindergarten!*" He leaned for-ward. "But never before have you deliberately at-tacked a boy for no reason."

Commando sat forward in shock. "I passed him the ball — it hit him in the face!"

"Yes," said Mr. Silverman sarcastically. "We always toss basketballs at people while they write. Don't lie, Armando. Douglas was bloody, and there *you* were. As usual."

"I was helping him out," Commando defended himself. "Trying to stop the bleeding."

The principal's gaze was icy. "Heaven protect us from your kind of helpfulness. This behavior is unacceptable. You need professional help — and I'm going to see that you get it. Every day at three-thirty."

Commando looked up. "I have basketball practice at three-thirty."

Mr. Silverman shook his head. "Until your fighting is under control, you're off the Minutemen."

Commando flushed red. "But I didn't do anything! Ask Doug!"

"That's enough," said the principal sternly. "This isn't a first offense. You've had ample warning."

"You don't care about me getting help," Commando accused bitterly. "You're just mad because Doug's dad's an ambassador!"

"That is ridiculous. Douglas Fairchild receives no special treatment here. Now, every day at three-thirty you are to go to the guidance office. See Mr. and Mrs. Richardson."

Commando's eyes widened in horror. "That's the *Twinkie Squad!*"

Waldo Turcott was devastated. "What do you *mean* you're off the team?"

Commando shrugged. "I'm just off. I can't play. Silverman said."

"But you're the best point guard in D.C.!"

"Well, I didn't exactly request this!" snapped Commando. "And let me tell you what else goes along with this package deal! While you guys are practicing, I'll be with the Special Discussion Group!"

Waldo's jaw dropped. "The Twinkie Squad? *You?* But you're a player, man!"

Commando laughed mirthlessly. "That was a lot of help while Silverman was nailing me!"

"I knew this would happen!" Waldo howled in agony. "I dreamt it!"

"Me getting kicked off the team?"

"It was — you know — symbolic," Waldo explained. "It started out great. I was in the low post against this guy, and he was nothing! I was muscling him all over the paint! Wide open, three feet from the hoop — *and no one passed me the ball!* See, that was you. *You* would have passed me the ball. But with you out, Kahlil plays point guard. And Kahlil couldn't pass a parked car in a Porsche!"

"Wait a minute!" he exclaimed suddenly. "All we have to do is get Coach Buckley to overrule Silverman's decision!"

"He can't," Commando pointed out. "Silverman's his boss."

Waldo stared at him. It was inconceivable to him that a principal could have more authority than a basketball coach.

"Kahlil's a ball hog," he moaned in true pain. "He takes forty-foot jumpers with men wide open, and he doesn't play defense, and he spends the whole warm-up styling his hair!"

"Look, I've got to go," said Commando. "I can't keep my fellow Twinkies waiting."

"Try some butt-kissing!" Waldo advised desperately. "Promise to be a good little boy, lie like crazy, and maybe they'll let you back on the Minutemen!"

From the doorway of the conference room, Commando shot Douglas a look that would have melted lead. Douglas merely sat, his expression blank.

The Richardsons, as usual, were smiling, and it got on Commando's nerves from the very first second.

"There's a guy out there," observed Ric Ewchuk, shifting from side to side in his chair.

Julia Richardson stood up. "You must be Armando," she beamed. "Welcome to the Special Discussion Group. I'm Julia, and my husband's name is Martin. Sit down and tell us about yourself."

Commando pulled up a chair and sat, folding his arms defiantly in front of him. "They told me I gotta come here at three-thirty," he said evenly. "Nobody said I gotta talk."

This made not a dent in the Richardsons' smiles. It seemed to Commando that if Thaddeus G. Little burned to the ground around them, Martin and Julia would be smiling right to the end.

"You have to talk, Armando," Mr. Richardson said gently. "If you don't participate, how will we make any progress with your problem?"

"I don't have a problem," said Commando evenly. "At least, I didn't till I walked in that door."

"Now, now," Julia chided. "We all have problems. Some of us are struggling in our classes, some of us don't mix well with fellow students, some of us have behavior problems — "

As she spoke, Commando gritted his teeth, lips pressed together in a thin line. He had vowed not to contribute one word to the Twinkie Squad, but he couldn't hold back. The Richardsons had asked for it, and they were going to get it.

"You want problems?" he exploded suddenly. "For starters, try 'Special Discussion Group'! There are about twenty things in this school called 'special,' and not one of them means anything good! Who are you kidding? You're the Twinkie Squad!" His face twisted. "*We're* the Twinkie Squad!"

Julia bristled. "We do not use that word here."

"Yeah?" challenged Commando. "Well, maybe you're the one who needs a counsellor, because you're fooling yourself. Everyone else in this building knows who we are!"

"Now, Armando — " began Martin.

"We're not here because we want to be here," Commando went on, as though no one had spoken. "We're here because we have no choice. You talk about not mixing well with everybody else. Well, when do all the sports and clubs and activities go on in this school? In the forty-five minutes after three-thirty when we're stuck in *here*! So don't look at *me* if you want problems! Maybe you should look in the mirror!" He sat back in his chair, sticking out his chin defiantly. He noticed in some amazement that Martin and Julia were still smiling.

"That's excellent," Martin approved. "You had all that anger, and you brought it out."

"It's not anger," insisted Commando. "It's the truth."

The other students were looking at the newcomer with awed respect.

Douglas spoke first. "Well, it's pretty obvious what we have to do."

Everyone stared. There was an expectant silence.
"We have to turn our group into a social organization," he went on. "Meetings would still be held
here at three-thirty — "

Martin cut in. "Douglas, as your guidance counsellors — "

"Oh, social clubs don't have guidance counsellors," Douglas reminded him. "We'll need another
title for you two. Perhaps 'associate members' —
nonvoting, of course."

"Voting?" Julia questioned.

"Well, yes, we're a democratic organization. We'll
have to elect a president and vice president, secretary, treasurer — naturally, the less important roles
would go to the associate members."

Martin stood up and faced Douglas. "It's a — great
idea, but it doesn't make any sense. We're a counseling group."

Douglas spread his hands questioningly. "It has
just been clearly explained that the group doesn't
work in its present format."

Commando groaned. "Shut up, Doug."

The pen that Ric had been gnawing on chose that
moment to disintegrate. All at once, his white turtle-
neck was covered in bright blue ink.

Dave laughed out loud. "Ha! I knew that was going
to happen!"

Anita laughed right along with him until Ric demanded, "What's so funny?"

She looked at him in shock. "Nothing."

"I once saw a movie about a psychotic killer who
goes around stabbing people with a fountain pen,"
put in Yolanda. "It was called *The Pen Is Mightier
Than the Sword*. Real scary!"

"Go clean up," Julia told Ric.

Before the word *up* had passed her lips, Ric was out the door as though he'd been fired from a cannon. They could hear his footsteps pounding down the hall as he headed for the bathroom in a full sprint.

For Commando, it was the longest forty-five minutes of his life. As far as he was concerned, all the rumors about the Special Discussion Group went *double*. How could anyone confine him in a small room with these — *Twinkies*? Dave, who hated everything in the world; Anita, who didn't have enough personality to form her own opinions; Ric, the human Mexican jumping bean; Yolanda, who was so wrapped up in the world of movies that she didn't have time for real life; Gerald, who might have been a nice guy, but who could tell? He hardly even looked up, let alone spoke.

And Doug. Commando had already reached a decision about Douglas Fairchild. Since Commando was already serving punishment for beating up Doug, he might as well earn it. Nothing spectacular — just one quick punch right where the basketball had nailed him. Doug sure deserved that and more for not telling Mr. Silverman what had really happened in the schoolyard.

At four-fifteen, the moment came. "Hey, Fairchild."

Douglas wheeled in front of his open locker.

Commando's voice was laced with sarcasm. "Thanks for helping me out with Silverman."

Douglas looked confused. "You're welcome," he said, and returned his attention to his locker.

Commando reached way up and spun the taller boy around. "You're a real funny guy, Doug. No wonder you're such a big hit on the Twinkie Squad. You've got my vote for head Twinkie."

Douglas regarded him. "Is there a problem?"

"I'm off the team!" raged Commando. "That's the only halfway decent thing I do in this school! I'm on the Twinkie Squad! And it's all your fault!"

Now Douglas was completely mystified.

"How dumb can a guy be?" cried Commando at the ceiling. He glared at Douglas. "Why didn't you tell Silverman I didn't do anything?"

"What didn't you do?"

"I didn't punch you in the face!" Commando exploded. "I'm on the Twinkie Squad because Silverman thinks I popped you one at recess!"

"But why would he think that?"

Commando was bitter. "Because your dumb nose was bleeding. And when it comes down to the ambassador's son, or the nobody who gets into fights and wears an earring, guess who takes the fall!"

Douglas started for the office, taking long strides so that Commando had to scramble to keep up.

The outer office was empty, so Douglas knocked lightly on the door marked PRINCIPAL.

"Douglas," said Mr. Silverman, rising from his chair. "And Armando," he added, without enthusiasm. "What can I do for you?"

"Sir, there's been a mistake," Douglas began briskly. "Armando never punched me. It was a mishap with the basketball. So there's no reason for him to be in the Special Discussion Group."

Mr. Silverman regarded them, shaking his head gravely. "Don't you think I know what's going on here? I was in middle school once, too, you know, and I understand how things work."

"Well," Douglas admitted, "it was somewhat improper of him to throw me the ball, knowing as he did that I'm a Pefkakian, and — "

The principal turned to Commando. "How dare you threaten Douglas into lying to try to get you off the hook?"

Commando stared. "I didn't threaten him! It's the truth!"

"I know the code of the schoolyard, Armando," Mr. Silverman informed them. "A boy with a bloody nose, or a black eye, claiming he walked into a door. Well, not in *my* school!"

"Sir, why won't you listen to me?" Douglas pleaded. "I was working on my history of Pefkakia, and naturally, I couldn't put it down, so I was defenseless when the ball — "

"You may think you're doing Armando a favor," the principal told Douglas. "But you're not. He'll have to get his behavior under control sooner or later. And now, boys, this interview is over."

Once in the hall, Commando turned furious eyes on Douglas. "Way to go, Doug! That was a big help!"

Douglas shrugged. "I tried to tell the truth."

Commando's shoulders twitched. Now was the time to haul off and lay Doug out. If Commando Rivera was going to be a Twinkie, he might as well deserve it.

But he couldn't. Sure, Doug was a jerk, but Commando simply could not hit a boy who wasn't a bully himself. Instead, he stormed away. He felt a hand grab his shoulder, and wheeled in anger. "Don't push your luck, kid!"

Douglas was regarding him earnestly. "I'm very sorry. I promise I'll get you out of this."

"Yeah? How?"

"I will prepare a piece of evidence so convincing, so irrefutable, that Mr. Silverman will have to accept it," Douglas vowed.

Commando stepped closer and, craning his neck, looked Douglas right in the eye. "I don't want any more favors! You've done enough already! I know it's not your fault Silverman's an idiot, but everything else is all thanks to you! There are five billion people on this planet, and you're the only one who wouldn't have caught that ball! I wish I'd never met you, man! You're the kiss of death! And if you want to keep your teeth, you'll stay out of my face!"

"Hey, Rivera, how does it feel to be a Twinkie?"

Commando didn't even look over his shoulder to identify his tormentor. He'd better get used to it, he thought grimly. The Twinkies got it all the time. He himself had thrown the occasional comment at them. He now regretted every word.

He took back alleys home, vaulting over garbage cans, and barking back at dogs. If this wasn't the worst day of his life, it was close. In the space of a few hours, he'd been accused of attacking an ambassador's son, kicked off the Minutemen, and sentenced to spend every afternoon shut in a small room with a gang of total Froot Loops.

He punched a tool shed. How could they group him with these nut cases? The answer was scary. In no time, he'd fit right in. Even if you were normal to start with, after a few weeks on the Twinkie Squad, you'd come out a Twinkie and a half!

The run home did nothing to calm him down. He was still shaking with rage as he scrambled up the

front steps. He was so disturbed that he was completely unprepared for the booby trap at the front
door. A string on the knob was connected to a giant
boom box. Opening the door flicked on the all-
heavy-metal station with the volume at full. The roar
of the music practically blasted him down the front
stairs and out into the street.

Cringing, he hit the "off" button, and quiet descended. Not complete quiet — he could hear the
shower running upstairs. Without hesitation, he
raced to the kitchen and twisted the hot-water tap
as far as it would go.

"*Yeeowww!*" came a cry from above. Turning on
the hot water left the shower ice-cold.

A few seconds later, Mr. Rivera, shivering in a track
suit, came running down the stairs. "You're early,
Comm. Short practice today?"

What practice? The whole sob story formed in
Commando's head. But then he looked at the dark
circles under his father's eyes — from studying all
night, and working all day, and going to school in
the evenings. Dad didn't really need to know that his
son was a Twinkie.

"Yeah, Dad. Short practice. And in answer to your
second question, I didn't write Mom, but I will tonight.
Whose turn to cook — yours or mine?"

"Burger King's," his father grinned. "Hey, how's
your friend the Pefkakian?"

Commando bit his tongue. "I don't see him
much."

Unbelievably, the thought of Douglas brought a
smile to Commando's lips. Stupid Doug, the cause
of all this mess, was the only guy on earth who might
be able to out-Twinkie the Twinkies. Even Martin

and Julia Richardson, who could smile through a nuclear winter, couldn't hack it once Doug started in on his Pefkakia routine. If there had been a good point in the afternoon, it was getting to see all those perfect teeth disappear behind two identical frowns.

"Are you going to let me in on the joke?" asked Mr. Rivera, smiling, too.

"It's nothing. I joined this new club at school."

4

The Grand Knights of the Exalted Karpoozi

"Here, Kahlil, I'll get that for you." Waldo was delicately balancing two trays through the crowded cafeteria line at lunch.

"Hey, no peas, man," said Kahlil. "I hate peas."

"Me, too," agreed Waldo. "Peas. Yeccch. Disgusting. Can I buy you dessert?"

Commando made a face. Waldo was so terrified that his new point guard wouldn't pass to him that he was turning himself into Kahlil's slave. He sidled up to Waldo. "I gave you twenty balls a game, and you never bought me a lousy stick of gum."

"Shhh!" hissed Waldo, indicating Kahlil. "He'll hear you!" The new point guard was trying to impress some seventh-grade girls by fake-dribbling a grapefruit up and down the cafeteria.

"You need the direct approach," whispered Commando. "Bend down, pucker up, and plant one right on his *derrière*."

"At least I'm not the one who walked out on the Minutemen!" Waldo accused.

"Hey, you want to step it up?" called Kahlil. "I'm starving. Got to get my energy to stomp Jefferson on Monday!"

"I hear Jefferson's got this six-foot-five seventh-grader," put in Commando. "They're pretty good."

"Jefferson's history!" Kahlil dismissed this. "*I'm* starting at point. Right, Turcott?"

"Right," agreed Waldo a little uneasily. Deep down, he would much rather have faced Jefferson with Commando handling the ball.

They made their way through the dining area, with Waldo carrying the extra tray. Kahlil led the way, continuing his antics with the grapefruit. He selected a table where Gerald Dooley sat alone, polishing off an entire page of math problems as he ate his sandwich. In one motion, Kahlil pulled the bench out from under the younger boy, depositing him on the floor, and handed him his brown bag lunch.

"Beat it, Twinkie. You're eating someplace else."

Commando dropped his tray, stepped over it, grabbed Kahlil by the collar, and pinned him backwards over the disputed table. "What are you — crazy? There are half a dozen empty tables!"

Waldo was horrified. He grabbed his old point guard and pulled him off his new point guard.

Kahlil dusted himself off. "You're brave, Rivera," he sneered.

"Oh, you, too!" returned Commando. "Picking on a ten-year-old kid! Too bad we don't have a kindergarten here, so you could *really* be a big man!"

Desperate to defuse the situation, Waldo wracked his brain to change the subject, and came up with basketball. "Did you guys catch the game on Channel S last night? The Tulsa Over-Sixty league? They've got this eighty-five-year-old who can jam!"

Glancing at Kahlil, Commando set Gerald back at the table. "Sorry, kid. Ignore the jerk."

"Thanks," Gerald murmured shyly. "See you at three-thirty."

Kahlil lifted six inches off the floor. *"Three-thirty!?"* He looked from Gerald to Commando. "Rivera, you're on the *Twinkie Squad?*"

Commando felt the hairs on the back of his neck curling. He could hear shuffling as students turned in their seats to regard him.

Waldo put an iron grip on Commando's arm. "Don't kill him, man! He's the only point guard we've got left!"

But Kahlil wasn't through yet. He knew he had an audience. "I knew you were dumb, Rivera, but I never thought you were Twinkie material!"

Commando turned to Waldo. "Just one punch! A couple of teeth — that's all I ask!"

"He's bigger than you, and two years older!" Waldo whispered desperately.

"This is a two-way street, you know!" Commando raged. "If you want to keep your precious point guard alive, you get him off my back!"

Waldo tried to smile genially. "Hey, Kahlil, be a good guy and take it back."

"I don't want him to take it back!" Commando growled. "I want him to eat it — raw, red, and wrapped in barbed wire!"

Coach Buckley was the teacher on lunch duty. "Hey, Rivera," he called over. "You guys are all pals there, right? 'Cause if you're not, move."

Commando surveyed the cafeteria. The only person he knew — besides Ric Ewchuk, who was bouncing up and down at his seat so hard that the mixed vegetables on his plate were airborne — was Douglas Fairchild. Douglas was snapping his fingers and calling, "Waiter — waiter — " It would be a frosty Friday in July before Commando would, on purpose, sit with that guy! He moved over and joined Gerald.

"Sorry, Kahlil," said Commando sweetly. "I know how touchy you are about how you got to be the starting point guard. It must have been tough to play backup to a sixth-grader."

Kahlil's eyes bulged. *"What?"*

"He didn't mean it! It came out wrong!" Waldo babbled.

Kahlil leaned across the table. "You think you're better than me, don't you, Rivera?"

Commando shrugged. "I don't think things I already know."

Waldo looked at Commando pleadingly, and mouthed the words "Chill out."

"Let's settle it once and for all," challenged Kahlil. "You and me. One-on-one. After school."

Commando smiled. There was nothing he would rather do than wipe up Kahlil on the court and then, after they were through with basketball, wipe up the court with Kahlil. "Sure — " he began.

There was a commotion in the cafeteria. A loud voice proclaimed, "In Pefkakia I wouldn't pay five *trikas* for this gruel!" The voice of —

Doug. His fellow Twinkie. "You know I can't make it. I've got Special Discussion Group."

Kahlil nodded understandingly. "We can't let the psychos out of their padded cells."
Commando bit his tongue.

"You would've won."
At first Commando didn't even realize the words were directed at him. He was in "delay" mode — waiting until the last possible minute to enter Guidance. Then he saw Gerald Dooley.
"You would've won," Gerald repeated.
"Won what?"
"Against that Kahlil guy," said Gerald. "You could've beaten him."
"I've beaten him a hundred times," grinned Commando. "That's what makes him so mean."
"You missed an important history test to see that silly science-fiction movie," Martin Richardson was telling Yolanda inside the conference room.
"Greetings, earthling," the eighth-grader replied in a robotic tone.
"That was supposed to be twenty percent of your final grade," Julia pointed out, still smiling.
"Take me to your leader," said Yolanda.
Douglas breezed in.
"Ah, Douglas," said Julia. "You're going to be our topic of discussion for today."
"There isn't time," Douglas replied briskly. From the pocket of his book bag he produced a small stack of white printed cards and began to hand them out. "Our membership cards are ready."
"Membership cards?" repeated Mr. Richardson. "For what?"
"Our social organization," Douglas explained.

"What are we?" asked Commando irritably. "The Shriners?"

Martin looked over Gerald's shoulder at the card he was cradling as though he held delicate crystal. " 'The Grand Knights of the Exalted Karpoozi'?"

Douglas smiled with satisfaction. "Majestic, isn't it?"

"It's beautiful!" breathed Anita.

"It's nonsense!" roared Mr. Richardson.

"It's nonsense," Anita amended.

"I'll have you know, sir," said Douglas, much offended, "that it is a well-respected order in Pefkakian society. The Karpoozi is the river that runs by the birthplace of the immortal Ano Pefki."

"Sorry," mumbled Martin.

"That's quite all right," said Douglas generously. "You weren't to know." Actually, *karpoozi* had come up in his alphabet soup the day before.

In between flipping, and folding, and twisting, Ric managed to sneak a look at his card. "Hey, wait a minute! You got my name wrong!"

"It isn't Richard Ewchuk?" Douglas asked.

"It's Calvin."

Commando spoke up. "So why do they call you Ric?"

"It's short for Ricochet," Ric explained. "When I was a kid I was hyperactive, and my mom said I used to bounce off the walls."

"When did you do all this?" Julia asked Douglas. She could barely take her eyes off her own card, which specified, ASSOCIATE MEMBER — *NO* VOTING PRIVILEGES.

"My parents are giving a large dinner party in

honor of the Secretary-General of the U.N.," Douglas explained. "While the engraver was running off the invitations, I had these printed up."

"Look, Douglas," said Martin carefully, "we really appreciate all your work getting us these great — uh — cards — "

"You're welcome," Douglas acknowledged.

" — but all that talk about a social club — well, it was just that. Talk. And, well — "

"What he's trying to say is tough luck," Commando translated. "No knights of the grand whatever."

"Karpoozi," supplied Douglas with dignity.

"Sit down, Douglas," said Mrs. Richardson, opening a manila file folder. "I have some complaints from your teachers."

"I can't imagine what," said Douglas stiffly. "I haven't done anything."

"That's the main complaint," Martin conceded. "You do no homework, you do no classwork, and when you're supposed to be paying attention, you're writing in your binder."

"I'm working on a book," Douglas explained. "It's terribly important."

"So is your education," Martin insisted. "Do you know what your geography mark is right now, as we speak? You don't even have one. So far you haven't turned in one piece of gradable work."

"That would be a matter of concern," Douglas explained, "if I were an American student. However, I am Pefkakian, therefore other countries are almost totally unimportant to me."

"Well, just what *is* important in Pefkakia?" Julia demanded. Once again her smile was gone.

"Oh, many things," Douglas replied. "Frolicking, primarily."

"Ms. Abernathy also mentioned something about you making a lot of noise in math class," added Julia. "According to her, you snort like a bull!"

Douglas looked wounded. "I suffer from postnasal drip. It is a medical condition."

This logic had the Richardsons staring at each other helplessly. Finally, Julia dug down deep and found her smile. "We've got some news. The high school is opening up its new athletic building next Friday. I've signed us all up to be ushers."

"Ushering what?" Dave asked skeptically.

"Everyone," Martin replied. "Students, parents, alumni. They've invited the Class of 1942 to be special guests. Some of them haven't been back in fifty years! Imagine!"

"Who cares?" Dave complained. "It's the high school's gym, not ours."

"The middle school will be making full use of the new building," Martin assured him. "The Minutemen will play there from now on."

Commando winced.

At last it was four-fifteen, and the group filed out of Guidance. Commando knew the basketball team would be having a short workout before tonight's season's opener, and he didn't want to run into Kahlil. Punching out the last remaining point guard scant hours before tip-off would only earn him more time on the Twinkie Squad. He was halfway out the door when a hand on his shoulder stopped him. He wheeled to find himself facing Douglas Fairchild.

"You got a problem, Doug?" he asked belligerently.

"You have to come to my house," said Douglas. "We've got some work."

"Take a hike," said Commando sourly. He spent forty-five minutes a day with Doug — *thanks to Doug!* Extending that time by even a nanosecond was out of the question.

"But it's ready," Doug protested.

"What's ready — besides your brain, for the Smithsonian?"

"The irrefutable evidence — proof that you didn't attack me," said Douglas. "I have it at home, but we have to decide exactly how to proceed."

Commando was thunderstruck. "Proof? What proof? You said it right to Silverman's face! If he didn't believe that, what's left?"

Douglas smiled. "I can't explain it here."

Commando thought it over. What did this idiot have that he thought could get Commando off the Twinkie Squad and back on the basketball team? "Why does it have to be your house?" he asked finally. "Why can't you bring it here?"

"Trust me," said Douglas. "You don't flash a document like this around."

One thing decided it for Commando. This was a chance to see Anton Fairchild's *house* — the place where the great man lived, the chair he sat in, the table he ate at, maybe even the study, where his best diplomatic ideas were hatched! And as for Douglas' "evidence" — it would be good for a laugh.

So it was that the two boys rode the school bus through the neighborhoods around Thaddeus G. Little to the town homes and luxury apartment buildings where so many political Washingtonians lived.

"Look!" Commando pointed at a distinguished

man in his mid-fifties, with a ring of white hair around his bald head. In the lobby of Douglas' building, the man stopped at the security desk to pick up his mail. "It's Senator McComb from Idaho!"

Douglas nodded. "I wish he'd move, or lose an election, or something. His dog has the kind of shaggy fur that's murder on a postnasal drip."

They rode the private elevator up to the penthouse, and the housekeeper let them in. Mrs. Fairchild was off planning a charity ball, and the ambassador had meetings at the White House.

Douglas headed for the kitchen. "Want something to drink?"

"What? Oh, yeah. Sure." Commando was staring at his surroundings, overawed. It was the kind of apartment he'd always imagined real big shots lived in — huge, luxurious, filled with sumptuous furniture. Bright sunlight streamed in through elegantly draped windows. And the view — all of Washington stretched out before him — the Capitol, the monuments, the Mall.

Douglas grabbed two Cokes and a bag of chips, and led Commando off to his suite. Once the door was shut behind them, he drew a padded manila envelope out of his desk. From that, he lovingly pulled a thick sheet of cream-colored stationery.

Commando frowned. The page was blank, except for a scribbled signature. "So what?"

"Read the name," Douglas urged.

Commando stared at the paper. The writing was highly stylized, and almost impossible to make out, like a doctor's prescription. And then a very famous name jumped off the page at him. "That's the Surgeon General! Is it real?"

"Of course," said Douglas.

"Wow!" Commando couldn't take his eyes off the signature. "It's great!" he managed. "But what does it have to do with me?"

Douglas took the sheet, fitted it into the electric typewriter on his desk, and began to type:

MEMO

TO: Mr. Silverman, Principal,
           Thaddeus G. Little Middle School

FROM: The Surgeon General of the
           United States of America

I hereby certify that it is medically impossible for Armando Rivera to have punched Douglas Fairchild on September 29, 1992. The injury (though serious in light of the patient's postnasal drip) was probably caused by a basketball.

Commando's eyes bulged. "The Surgeon General *said* that?"

"Well, not in so many words," Douglas replied vaguely.

"Where did you get the signature?"

Douglas shrugged. "I told my dad I was doing a special project on the health department, and I needed the autograph for the cover."

"You can't do that!" Commando exploded. "You can't just take that signature and put any old thing down, like it was a Surgeon General's report! You could have typed *Lettuce causes brain damage,* or

The earth is flat, or *Two plus two equals five!"*

"But I didn't. I put that you didn't hit me, which is true, so what's the problem?" To emphasize this point, he typed *Yours very truly,* directly above the name.

"Look, Doug," said Commando faintly, "I appreciate your help, but there must be some kind of law against this. I mean, this is — like — *fraud!"*

"But it'll get you back on the basketball team," Douglas argued.

"Oh, man!" moaned Commando. "By the time we got out of jail, I'd be too *old* to play basketball! It's misusing the authority of the highest doctor in the country! We'd *fry!"*

Douglas looked disappointed. "But, you see, this is the only irrefutable evidence I have. If we don't use this, you'll have to stay in the Special Discussion Group."

"It's okay!" exclaimed Commando fervently. "I just don't want to go to jail!"

Douglas took the document back and returned it to his desk drawer. "If you change your mind, let me know. You'll notice I didn't date it."

There was an insistent knocking at the door. "Douglas!" came Mrs. Fairchild's voice. "Are you in there? Who ordered all that squid?"

Douglas leaned over to Commando. "Squid is a Pefkakian delicacy," he whispered.

Mrs. Fairchild entered. "Douglas, the doorman says there's eleven pounds of squid downstairs, packed in dry ice!" She spied his companion, and started. "I know you! You're Commando!"

"Right!" Commando exclaimed, thrilled. Then he recalled their first meeting — his nose dripping blood from the bout with Michael. "Nice to see you again, Mrs. Fairchild," he added sheepishly.

"Douglas, we'll discuss it later. And it better not have anything to do with Pefkakia." She turned her attention to the visitor. "Commando, we're having an early dinner tonight. Would you like to join us? We're not serving the squid," she added with a pointed look at her son. "That's going straight back to Nova Scotia!"

"Thank you very much," said Commando, "but it's my turn to cook at home. My dad's got night school. I'd better hurry."

"Do you live around here?" asked Mrs. Fairchild.

"No, our place is back by the school," Commando replied. "Is there a bus stop close by?"

"We'll send you with one of the cars," she decided. "I'll just go and call the garage."

Commando looked at Douglas nervously and received a reassuring smile. "There'll be a driver," Douglas said.

Douglas escorted Commando to the hall and called the elevator. When the door opened, there stood Ambassador Fairchild, briefcase in hand.

At the sight of the famous face, Commando forgot himself, and blurted out, "Ambassador Fairchild, what are you doing here?"

"I live here," the diplomat said plaintively. He scowled at his son. "There's a lot of squid down there marked *Fairchild*. I hope there are some other Fairchilds in this building."

"Dad, this is Commando from school."

The two shook hands, and Commando privately vowed never to wash his hand again. "I really got into your speech at the Rome Summit. They showed parts of it on *Political Diary*. I think you blew those European foreign ministers pretty much away."

The ambassador was taken aback. "You watched it on TV?"

Commando gazed worshipfully up at him. "I'm one of your biggest fans. You'll probably be going to Helsinki soon. We're sending a lot of our top people there."

Mr. Fairchild seemed to consider this. "Good to meet you." He gave Douglas a dirty look. "Come on. Let's talk squid."

David Rivera stepped out of the Metro station and trudged along G Street towards home. Here it was only Monday, and he had had enough of this week already. And the day wasn't over yet. He still had night school to deal with. Wearily, he placed one foot in front of the other. His briefcase weighed sixty tons.

He thought of the long blocks ahead. Maybe if he closed his eyes, he'd be whooshed to his own doorstep.

A long silver-gray stretch limousine whispered up to the curb beside him. The smoked glass of the passenger window descended with a quiet hum, and a familiar voice said, "Hey, peasant, you want a lift?"

David Rivera stared at his son, riding in air-conditioned leather luxury in the back of the limo. He climbed in beside Commando and accepted a Coke from the mini-bar.

"So, Dad, what do you think?"

Mr. Rivera toasted his son in cola. "Who died?"

5

Garlic Squid with Mango and Banana

The Thaddeus G. Little playground rocked with noisy activity. Portable stereos blared musical accompaniment to laughter, cheers, jeers, and arguments. It was eight-thirty, ten minutes before the start of first period, and the students were enjoying the last few moments of freedom until lunch.

One boy, however, seemed anxious to get to class. Douglas Fairchild strode purposefully from the last bus through the crowded schoolyard to the building. He ignored the main entrances, which were locked until eight-forty, and moved straight to the janitor's service door. He poked his head inside. "Mr. Stark?"

There was no answer.

He entered, and walked through the storage area and past another door, which put him in the school halls. Once inside, he navigated the deserted corridors down the stairs to the home ec room, which was on the basement level, directly below the office.

He peered in the door. Empty. Ms. Castlefield was probably in the staff room with the rest of the teachers. Perfect. His fellow members of the Special Discussion Group were having trouble getting the hang of being Grand Knights of the Exalted Karpoozi. Obviously, Douglas had sprung the membership cards on them too quickly, before they'd had time to get used to the idea. Well, today he would create the perfect atmosphere, by treating the Grand Knights to a lunch fit for a Pefkakian — garlic squid with mango and banana.

Of course, Douglas had no way of knowing if Pefkakians really did eat squid — or even if there were any squid in that part of the world. (And where exactly *was* that part of the world again?) The important thing was to turn Twinkies into Grand Knights. And besides, garlic squid couldn't be any worse than the usual slop they served in the cafeteria.

He reached into his backpack and pulled out a steaming paper bag — not hot steam, but the vapor produced by dry ice. He unpacked the parcel tenderly, placing the squid on the counter. He took a frying pan out of the cupboard, set it on the stove at low heat, and dropped in a pat of butter to melt. He peeled one of the bananas and began slicing it.

The bell rang, and Douglas froze. So late already? That incompetent bus driver hadn't gotten him to school in time to prepare the meal! In a panic, he packaged up the squid and fruit, and turned off the stove. He surveyed the room as marching feet began to sound out in the halls. He could hide his lunch for the morning, and cook it up, posing as a student, in fifth period. But where could he put it now? The fridge? Too obvious. The cupboards? No good

either. There would be four home ec classes in here
before he got back. In desperation, his eyes turned
upward, and there it was. A ceiling tile was missing,
one white square out of hundreds. Urgently, he
hopped up on a counter, reached up a long arm,
and placed the package into the hole and out of
sight. Then he jumped down and started out of the
room. Just as he was about to make good his escape, the door burst open, and in swaggered Kahlil,
leading the eighth-grade first-period home ec class.

"Look, a Twinkie!" announced the point guard in
exaggerated surprise.

"Aw, leave the kid alone," said Waldo wearily.

"If he wants to be in *our* classroom, he's got to
pay rent!" Kahlil grabbed Douglas' book bag and
held it high in the air.

Douglas flushed with annoyance. "Give me that."

"Dump it out!" cheered Beverly. "Let's see what
he's got!"

Kahlil emptied the contents of the backpack onto
the floor. From the pile of notebooks, rulers, and
pens, Beverly snatched up the yellow binder.

"Hey, great!" she cried. "Now we'll see what this
Twinkie writes!"

"Absolutely not!" Douglas thundered. "It isn't finished yet!"

With a nasty laugh, Kahlil dropped the bag,
grabbed the notebook from Beverly, backed up, and
tossed it high in the air towards Waldo.

With total concentration, Douglas launched himself straight up, reached out a long arm, and swatted
at the binder. He caught the bottom corner, tipping
it straight up. Then he gathered it in, and came down
with it fully in his grasp.

Waldo was bug-eyed. "He blocked your shot, man!" he exclaimed to Kahlil. "He can *sky!*"

"It was goaltending," mumbled Kahlil. He placed a sneaker-clad foot on Douglas' bag. "You want your stuff? Come and get it."

Just then the P.A. system sprang to life. *"Good morning,"* came Mr. Silverman's voice. *"Just one announcement. Last night the Thaddeus G. Little Minutemen played a great game, but came up just short against Jefferson, losing 71 to 38."*

This public announcement of yesterday's humiliating defeat seemed to take all the energy out of everybody. Kahlil stepped off the backpack, and took a seat, muttering under his breath. Waldo helped Douglas stuff his belongings into his bag.

"Great block, kid," Waldo whispered. Then he took his seat with his friends.

Douglas watched the clock all through fourth period. He felt a little extra hungry today, which he figured was a lot like the Pefkakians must feel before their famous squid festivals(?).

He had deliberately taken a seat by the door in order to ensure that he would be the first one out of class and racing down to the basement. The rumble of moving feet was everywhere. Class was over, and here was Mr. Maushart, rambling on and on about the plight of East Coast fishermen. How was life supposed to get any better for East Coast fishermen if people couldn't get to their squid because of some blowhard talking all through the lunch hour?

Quietly, Douglas closed his binder and attempted to finesse his way out the door.

"Hungry, are we, Douglas?" Mr. Maushart was

glaring at him. He glanced at the clock. "I suppose you're right. Okay. Dismissed, everybody." Douglas took off like a bullet.

He burst out of the stairwell on the basement level, and surveyed the situation. A line of students filed out of the home ec room, followed by Ms. Castlefield. Perfect timing. He waited until they were out of sight, then ducked into the room.

He had tiptoed halfway across the floor before he realized that he was not alone. Two workmen stood there. One of them was watching Douglas in amusement; the other was atop a stepladder, plastering in a brand-new replacement ceiling tile.

Douglas looked up at where he knew his squid feast was trapped forever. "Hmmm."

The man on the ladder looked down. "Can we do something for you, kid?"

"I don't suppose those tiles are removable?" said Douglas hopefully.

"Nope. Permanent."

He ate a miserable lunch in the cafeteria, but his heart was in the ceiling of the home ec room.

In sixth-period science class, Mr. Poppolini was discussing the migratory habits of the wildebeest. Douglas raised his hand.

"Sir, how long does it take for dry ice to evaporate?"

Mr. Poppolini stared. "What does that have to do with the wildebeest?"

"Well," said Douglas, "let's say you had some wildebeest steaks packed in dry ice. How long would they stay fresh?"

"So long as it fits into our topic," the teacher said sarcastically. "I don't know. Depending on how much dry ice you have, maybe twelve hours at room temperature. Okay?"

"Thanks," said Douglas. It meant that around eight o'clock tonight, the dry ice would be gone, and the lost lunch would be on its own. And judging by the sturdiness of those tiles, that squid was going to be there a lot longer than twelve hours.

Coach Buckley was becoming exasperated. "Aw, come on, Fairchild, just jump over the stupid thing!"

Douglas was on his hands and knees, inspecting the vaulting horse. "Shouldn't there be some sticker to indicate that it's been safety-tested?"

Buckley slapped his forehead. "Every school in the country has one of these! Ten million kids a day jump 'em! And no one makes a big deal about it!"

Amid scattered applause from his fellow students, Douglas loped to the front of the line. There he stood, poised like a pole vaulter, taking deep breaths.

"Hurry up, Fairchild! It's not a trip to the moon! They've got air on the other side!"

Douglas began his limbering-up exercises, starting with stretches, and working up to deep knee-bends and jumping jacks.

"Come on!" roared the coach.

Obediently, Douglas ran in place for a moment, then sprinted three giant steps towards the apparatus. He hit the takeoff point, and froze, like a baby gooney bird poised for its first flight.

"Now what?"

"I'm judging the distance," Douglas explained. "Ski jumpers do it all the time."

The coach was purple with rage. "You've got five seconds to get over that vaulting horse, or I'll be judging the distance between my foot and the seat of your pants!"

But just as Douglas was about to make another run at the horse, the intercom sprang to life.

"Coach Buckley, could you send Douglas Fairchild to the guidance office, please."

"Dead or alive?" the coach choked.

"Alive, please. Mr. and Mrs. Richardson want to see him."

Douglas gazed at the vaulting horse with regret. "Too bad. I think I was working up a good vault — for a Pefkakian." He changed into his regular clothes, and ambled off towards Guidance.

The Richardsons were waiting for him in the hall, their smiles already strained. "All right, Douglas, what's this?" Martin was pointing at a large notice tacked to the bulletin board. It read:

SIGN UP HERE FOR
THE GRAND KNIGHTS OF
THE EXALTED KARPOOZI

Underneath there were fifty sign-up lines, but no signatures.

"Don't try to tell us this isn't your doing," Julia persisted. "Who else would use Roman numerals?"

"But what's the problem?" asked Douglas. "Did I misspell 'Karpoozi'?" He squinted at the sheet.

"The problem is there are no Grand Knights!" Martin exploded, ripping the paper violently from the board. "Why can't you accept it? Haven't you noticed the only person who even talks about it is *you*?"

Douglas was horrified. "Sir, you have to put that back!"

"Douglas, be serious," Julia said reasonably. "What if someone put his name on that sheet?"

"That's the beauty of it," was Douglas' argument. "No one *will* sign up, since they know nothing about us, and won't be able to find out."

Mr. Richardson threw his arms up. "So what's the point of having a sign-up sheet?"

"Don't you see the symbolism?" Douglas cried in disbelief. "The sign-up sheet makes us a club. Without it, we're prisoners —"

"Douglas!" exclaimed Julia.

"Are we there of our own free will?" asked Douglas. "Can we leave if we choose?"

"Come on," groaned Martin. "If that's your logic, all students are prisoners."

"Not exactly," Douglas pointed out. *"Everybody* has to go to school. But we're singled out for Special Discussion Group. That is — unless we have a sign-up sheet."

"Oh, yeah? Well, here's your sign-up sheet!" Martin tore the paper into sixteenths, and dropped the scraps into Douglas' cupped hands. Then he led his wife into the office.

"See you at three-thirty," added Julia, smiling once again.

Clucking sadly, Douglas carried the scraps of the sign-up sheet to the office. Mr. Silverman was doing some paperwork at the counter. He looked up and smiled. "What can I do for you, Douglas?"

"Could I have some Scotch tape, please?" Douglas requested.

Yes, the repaired sign-up sheet was ugly — it looked like a paper-and-tape chessboard made by a three-year-old. But it was a symbol. And, after all, no one was ever going to put a name on it.

He nestled it carefully between a cheerleading notice and an ad for cheap piano lessons. He smiled
with satisfaction. Unless they were looking for it, the
Richardsons would never know it was up there again.

Absolutely nothing was accomplished in Special
Discussion Group that day because Anita Ditmar
had a new haircut.

"How do you like it?" She threw the question open
to everyone, modelling nervously.

"It looks like a bird's nest!" snorted Dave.

"Dave!" exclaimed Mr. Richardson in horror.

But Anita was already in a rage. "I know!" she
agreed fervently. "I almost strangled the stylist! I can't
believe they had the nerve to take my money."

"Nonsense, *dah*ling, it's *mah*vellous!" put in Yolanda in a snobby, aristocratic tone. "Simply divine!"

"What a lovely thing to say," approved Julia.

Commando laughed in her face. "*Manhattan Society Ladies* is the new movie at the Marquis."

Yolanda nodded enthusiastically. "Yes, *dah*ling,
you *must* see it! It's a *mah*-sterpiece of *aht*!"

This went on for twenty minutes, with Anita threat-
ening to shave her head bald and wear wigs. Finally,
Martin laid down the law, still smiling. "Anita, your
hair looks fine. Now, can we please get started?"

That was when Ric, who had been tipping his chair
back on the two rear legs, shoved a little too hard.
He keeled over backwards, landing with a tremen-
dous crash on the floor, knocking himself silly.

Dave Dunn found this so hilarious that he put his
head down on the table and howled with laughter.

"*Dah*ling, call an *ah*mbulance," cried Yolanda. "Call a *pah-rah*-medic!"

Martin squatted down to examine Ric.

"Is he dead?" ventured Gerald timidly.

That was it for Dave. He fell off his chair and rolled on the floor beside Ric, rollicking with mirth.

Commando stared in disgust. "Are you crazy, man? The kid could be really hurt!"

At that moment, Ric's eyelids fluttered, and he sat up. "Mr. Richardson! What are we doing down here?"

Douglas regarded Julia earnestly. "Now do you see why we have to change the format of the group?"

But by that time, Mr. Richardson had managed to haul Ric to his feet, and was trying to steer him towards Nurse Chung's office, so the Special Discussion Group was canceled for the day.

As they filtered out into the hall, Commando started towards Douglas, and hesitated. Okay, it was Doug, and all this was his fault. But he didn't mean to be such a jerk. And he *had* tried to get Commando back on the team. Besides, Doug had invited him over, offered dinner, and then sent him home in a stretch limo. Commando should at least *try* to return the favor.

"Hey, Doug, got any plans?"

Douglas regarded him suspiciously. "I'm going home."

"Why don't you come over to my place?" Commando suggested. "Maybe hang for dinner?"

Douglas brightened. "You've decided to use the irrefutable evidence!"

"No!" Commando exclaimed. "No. I just figured — since I've been over at your house — "

"My time is limited," Douglas pointed out. He hefted his yellow binder. "My history of Pefkakia has suffered a number of setbacks — "

"Just forget it," Commando interrupted with a sigh of exasperation. "I'll see you around." He headed out the door. It was stupid to think that Doug participated in the kind of stuff *humans* did. Commando felt silly for even considering it.

Once at home, he plopped down in front of the TV, switching channels. The videos were mostly teeny-bopper stuff in the after-school time slot, so he switched over to *Political Diary*. They were re-running Ambassador Anton Fairchild's historic speech at the Rome Summit. Commando shook his head. It was impossible to believe that the brilliant diplomat could have anything to do with *Doug!*

In the stack of mail on the coffee table, Commando caught sight of a Thaddeus G. Little envelope. His mind raced:

1. It was addressed to his father.

2. It was from Silverman, probably informing Mr. Rivera about the Minutemen and the Twinkie Squad.

Number 2 beat out 1. Commando threw the letter, unopened, into the garbage.

The living room vibrated with a low twangy sound. Commando pulled up short, feeling guilty. His father was home early. The noise came from the ancient wrought-iron railing on the front steps. (Their upstairs neighbor worked the late shift, and the gonging of the handrail woke the Rivera household up without fail every night at one A.M.)

He ran to the kitchen, pulled a pail from under the sink, and half-filled it with water. Keeping the bucket steady, he sprinted back through the living room to the front hall, and opened the door just a crack. He delicately balanced the bucket on the edge, and flattened himself against the wall. It was a pretty obvious booby trap; Dad would never fall for it in a million years. Still, on such short notice, it was the best he could do.

There were approaching footsteps, then — the doorbell? Why would David Rivera need to ring his own bell? Dad was up to something.

Slowly — agonizingly slowly — the door began to open. The bucket of water didn't fall. *It stayed balanced on the top of the door!*

A head poked inside. "Hello? Anybody home?"

"Doug?" Commando ran up to him. "What are you doing here?"

"I was invited," said Douglas, stepping inside. As he opened the door the rest of the way, the bucket wobbled and fell, right on Commando!

Douglas was bug-eyed. "What was that?"

"I thought you were my dad," sputtered Commando, drenched from head to toe.

"Are you trying to *drown* him?"

"Oh, we always booby-trap each other." Commando wrung out his shirt. "It's this thing we've got going. I nail him, he zonks me. It's not serious. I mean, we don't hate each other, or anything."

Douglas regarded the top of the door skeptically. "Not very creative."

"I'd like to see you do better," countered Commando, squishing on soaked high-tops to the bathroom in search of a towel.

Douglas looked thoughtful. "Have you considered a decoy?"

Commando emerged, drying his earring with toilet paper. "Decoy?"

Douglas smiled knowingly. "Fill up the bucket."

Two figures crouched in readiness at the top of the stairs.

"You know," mused Douglas, "I think this is a lot like the excitement and playful exhilaration Pefkak- ians feel while frolicking amidst the bullrushes."

Commando rolled his eyes. "It's five-thirty. My dad should be here any minute. Hey, Doug, how'd you find out where I live?"

"The school secretary gave me your address. She's incompetent, of course. I could have been a terrorist, or an axe murderer."

Commando had to laugh. "She probably noticed you're a sixth-grader." Suddenly, he froze. The sound of the iron banister gonged all around the living room. "It's him. Get ready."

Mr. Rivera easily spotted the pail at the front door. He disarmed the booby trap and pushed open the door. "Comm?" he called. "You're slipping, kid."

No answer.

He put down the bucket and headed for the stairs. "Hey, Comm, better luck next time — "

"Now!" cried Commando.

As David Rivera hit the bottom step, an enormous king-size bedspread descended from above, cov- ering him completely. The forty soda cans Com- mando and Douglas had tied to the fringed edges landed with a clatter. Struggling to free himself, Mr. Rivera lost his balance, and fell heavily to the floor in a cacophony of soft-drink containers against hard- wood. There, he continued to thrash and squirm.

Commando flashed Douglas the thumbs-up signal, then turned his attention below. "Uh — Dad?"

"What?" asked the bedspread.

"Do you want us to get you out?"

"I can do it." The crashing resumed.

"Come on," Commando grinned at Douglas. "I can't stand the noise."

They ran down the stairs and flung the bedspread from their captive. Mr. Rivera jumped to his feet and attempted to dust off his navy-blue suit, which was now hopelessly wrinkled and lint-covered.

Smiling, he slapped Commando on the shoulder. "Good one!"

"The decoy part was Doug's idea," Commando admitted. "I told you who his dad is — "

"Hey, great!" interrupted his father, pumping Douglas' hand. "I've never met a Pefkakian before."

"There aren't a whole lot of us living abroad," beamed Douglas.

Mr. Rivera turned to his son. "I don't suppose you guys gave a thought to dinner while you were plotting to murder me."

"I've got it covered," replied Commando, motioning towards the kitchen. "Doug and I made a pot of killer chili. Wait till you taste it! We just have to get these cans back to the recycling bin."

Dinner was a success. Douglas downed three bowls of the fiery chili; the Riveras each had two.

Mr. Rivera opened his belt buckle a notch. "That was great, guys! Is that Pefkakian-style chili?"

"Oh, no," said Douglas. "Our spicy tastes lean towards squid."

Commando's father raised an eyebrow. "I never knew Pefkakia was on the water. What ocean?"

Douglas looked completely blank. His Pefkakian geography was a zero.

"Oh, hey — " Mr. Rivera turned to his son. "Listen, Comm, I figured out why you didn't tell me about your first basketball game."

Commando choked on the last mouthful of chili. *"What?!"* he rasped as Douglas pounded his back.

"Seventy-one to thirty-eight!" exclaimed Mr. Rivera. "I guess the other team was pretty tough."

Douglas looked surprised. "But Mr. Rivera, don't you know — ?"

Under the table, Commando kicked Douglas hard enough to splinter steel. "I figured you wouldn't want to hear about it," he told his father quickly. "It wasn't exactly a barn-burner."

"That's because you didn't have me cheering you on." Mr. Rivera stood up. "Things are rough with my exams coming up. But as soon as I'm a CPA, I promise I'll be at every game."

Commando smiled weakly. "Great, Dad."

"My father has a friend who's a CPA," put in Douglas. He frowned. "Wait a minute — I think he's the Secretary of the Treasury."

"Well, I'm history," said Mr. Rivera. "Hope my chili breath doesn't scorch the professor." He grabbed an armload of books and headed for the door. The phone rang. Books under his arm, jacket slung over his shoulder, he picked up the receiver and jammed it under his chin. "Hello? . . . Yeah, sure, he's here . . . *who?* . . . yeah, no problem. He'll be waiting." He hung up, mouth agape.

"Who was it?" asked Commando.

His father stared at Douglas in awe and wonder.

"That was the FBI. Didn't you call your mom to let her know you were here?"

Douglas nodded sagely. "Ah, yes, the American need to keep tabs on your relatives. We Pefkakians are much more easygoing."

"In other words, he didn't call her," translated Commando with a snicker.

"I forgot," Douglas admitted.

6

Judging a Great Man by His Socks

Mr. Silverman stood in the bathroom of his office, gazing into the mirror at his sparse beard. He reached up with a small scissors, trimmed a few stray hairs, and then studied the effect. Not bad.

He stepped out of the bathroom, pulled his jacket off the clothes tree, and shrugged into it. He paused, nose twitching. There was a peculiar smell in here — kind of fishy, but sort of like rotten fruit, too. He checked the wastebasket. Perfectly clean. He began pulling at his desk drawers and peering inside. He'd once left an egg sandwich in there for two semesters. He even opened the filing cabinet. Nothing. He sniffed again. Yes, there was definitely something smelly around here. But there was no time to investigate further. He was already late for the opening of the new athletic building at the high school. He would mention it to Mr. Stark first thing Monday.

What Mr. Silverman didn't know was that nothing

in his office was causing the mysterious odor. It was coming from below his office — more specifically, from the ceiling of the home ec room on the basement level beneath him. There the ingredients for Pefkakian garlic squid with mango and banana had already begun to rot.

Beverly Busby, resplendent in her gold Thaddeus G. Little cheerleading outfit, scowled at the members of the Special Discussion Group.

"Why did they bring the Twinkie Squad?" she seethed. "The alumni will think we're all crazy!"

Carol Stefanovich, also a cheerleader, laughed. "Lighten up, Bev. They're just ushers. A baboon could do it."

"We're not talking about baboons; we're talking about Twinkies! That Fairchild idiot, for one!"

"Let's let them do their thing, and we'll concentrate on ours," said Carol.

Waldo jogged up, gym bag over his shoulder. The Minutemen were scheduled to play a game as an introduction to the main event, which was the Washington High game. "Hey, guys, what's up?"

With a grimace, Beverly gestured towards the Special Discussion Group. "Twinkie alert."

Waldo spied Commando, and brightened. He was about to call to his old friend when Kahlil's voice reached him. "Yo, Turcott. Carry my sneakers."

Painfully, Waldo turned. Kahlil had backed a girl against the wall, and was rapping away while holding out his gym shoes by their dirty laces.

Carol read Waldo's mind. "He's not going to pass to you anyway. Let him carry his own shoes."

But to Waldo, nothing was more important than

basketball. He snatched the shoes from Kahlil's hand, and marched to the locker room, ears burning.

Mr. Hagen, the high school's vice principal, sidled up to Mr. Richardson. "Brace yourself, Martin. We're seven short."

"Seven what?"

"Tour guides. Seven kids didn't show up. I guess we'll have to cancel the tour — "

"Of course you won't!" Julia interrupted. "We've got seven extra guides right here."

Mr. Hagen looked around excitedly. "Where?"

"Right here!" snapped Julia. "*Our* kids!"

The vice principal deflated like a balloon. "Oh. Well — uh — thanks, but — "

"What's wrong with our group?" Julia demanded.

"Well — " Mr. Hagen hemmed and hawed. "They don't have the — uh — *experience* — "

"And the others have all led tours through the pyramids, I suppose!" Martin chimed in. He turned to the group. "Good news, people. We're going to fill in as alumni tour guides."

Gerald's eyes opened wide as saucers. "Now?" His voice was just a whisper.

"Of course, now!" barked Mr. Hagen, handing out building maps to the seven new guides. "The arrows show exactly where you should take your group. All information about the complex and its features is right there. Got it?"

Douglas spoke up. "I don't suppose you have a medieval biathlon fletzel in here."

Mr. Hagen gawked. "A *what?*"

"That's where you conduct a medieval biathlon. On a fletzel." He added, "I'm a Pefkakian."

Mr. Hagen looked at the Richardsons. "Maybe we should cancel the tour."

But at that moment, the fifty-four members of the Class of '42 began to file in.

Beverly gawked as the Special Discussion Group was led over to the small cluster of tour guides. "They're letting *Twinkies* run the tour?" she gasped in horror. "No!"

"Now remember, these people are elderly," Julia whispered, as the guests were formed into clusters of five. "So walk slowly, and speak distinctly."

Gerald Dooley was first. Without a word of introduction, he zoomed off towards the pool, leaving his bewildered group staring after him. He was past the high-diving board before Martin ran him down.

Dave took the next group, and he was a lot more talkative, if not friendly. "Personally, I think this place is stupid. No offense, but that's just one guy's opinion. Like the pool. Big deal. . . ." And he led his group off to the pool behind Gerald, who was mumbling out a running commentary:

"This is the pool . . . it's got water in it . . . it's for swimming."

Yolanda showed the most enthusiasm. "Welcome, *dah*-lings, to this *mah*-vellous ex-*ah*-mple of *ah*-chitecture."

Meanwhile, Ric, his head sporting a large lump from yesterday's spill, was taking care of business.

"Okay, first things first. Who's gotta go to the bathroom?" There was no response from his bewildered tour group. Ric rolled up his building map, and began banging it on his knee. "Come on! There's no turning back once we get started!"

A traffic jam was forming, and the Richardsons were forced to intervene. Finally, the four high-school tour guides were sent ahead with their groups, followed by Anita, Commando, and Douglas. Ric's group was off on a bathroom break, and would bring up the rear.

Douglas led his five ladies and gentlemen through the doorway to the pool area. But then, instead of following Commando, he made a sharp left turn, and directed them to a stairwell leading to the basement. "This way, folks. I'll join you at the bottom."

"Pssst! Doug! What're you doing?" Commando was stopped dead, staring at him.

"Conducting the alumni tour," replied Douglas.

"But the tour goes this way!"

Douglas smiled. "We're expected to show these people the obvious — a pool, a weight room, a basketball court. I think we should give these alumni credit for a little more depth and sophistication."

"Yeah, but the *basement*!?"

"To judge this building by its basketball court," Douglas explained patiently, "is like judging a great man by his socks. The true character comes out in the guts and the heart. And that's in the basement."

"Come on, son," a white-haired gentleman called to Commando. "I don't want to miss the game."

Commando backed away. "I hope you know what you're doing."

Douglas smiled again. "Don't I always?"

Commando stared. Now was probably a bad time to mention the Surgeon General's letter.

The basement was damp and cold, and smelled of fresh paint. Glaring fluorescent lights illuminated a brand-new world of blah. The floor, the walls, the ceiling, even the ducts and pipes, were painted exactly the same shade of battleship gray.

The ceiling was low. Douglas took two steps forward and banged his head on a pipe. Reeling, he hung onto the wall. "This," he began dramatically, "is the true nerve center of the Washington High School Sports Complex."

"Where's the basketball court?" asked Mr. Buckingham, a short, well-preserved gentleman who looked like Albert Einstein.

"Without all this, there could *be* no basketball court!" Douglas explained. "Look! The air-conditioning compressor! And now" — he led them through a reinforced steel door marked *KEEP OUT* — "the furnace room!"

Mrs. Dupuis looked around dubiously. "When do we get to see the Nautilus machines?"

"Providing heat for this entire huge building!" Douglas announced grandly. "But what heats the pool, you're probably asking yourself? Ta-da!" He pointed to a second furnace. "There it is — the pool heater!"

Mrs. Dupuis' husband, a retired army colonel who was in full-dress uniform, including a chestful of medals and ribbons, spoke up. "Now, just a moment, young man. We didn't come here to change a fuse. Let's get on with the tour."

"Certainly, sir. This way, ladies and gentlemen."

Mr. Buckingham banged his knee on a standing pipe. "Yeow!"

"Careful, sir," said Douglas cheerfully, herding his people down a long, dark corridor. "Now, you've probably heard that the field house alone has seating for more than three thousand people."

"This is more like it," said Colonel Dupuis.

"A crowd that size can produce a great deal of garbage," Douglas went on. "You see before you the trash compactor, capable of reducing tons of refuse into neat, manageable parcels."

Miss Dalrymple, a frail little creature in a smart linen suit, scowled at Douglas. "Young man, I did not drive all the way from Baltimore to be taken on a tour of the garbage!"

"All the other people are getting the real thing," added Mrs. Dupuis sulkily. "Why are we prowling around in the cellar?"

"But don't you feel it?" raved Douglas. "It's all around you!"

"Feel what?" asked the colonel irritably.

"The heartbeat of the building! The life force! The power hum! All that stuff like the swimming pool and the basketball court is just window-dressing, like having the right designer label on your T-shirt! This is the real thing! See it! Hear it! Feel it! Smell it!"

"All I smell is garbage," growled Mr. Cuccina. "Get us out of here."

"All right," sighed Douglas. "Just let me show you one more thing! I've saved the best for last!"

"*Then* can we go on the normal tour?" Miss Dalrymple persisted.

"Certainly," said Douglas. "But for now — follow me, and prepare to be astounded!"

Like a man on a mission, he led them through a maze of corridors, deeper into the bowels of the basement. The ceiling was lower. There were more pipes jutting out at odd angles. The cement floor seemed to slope downward.

"We're going down!" complained Mrs. Dupuis.

She turned to her husband. "Make him stop!"

"Now, see here, son!" the colonel exploded. "Do you know where you're going? We've made an awful lot of turns."

"We're almost there," Douglas promised. He increased his pace, striding ahead to stand proudly beside a hole in the floor that was surrounded by a small metal railing.

"If that's the sewer, I don't want to know about it," said Mr. Cuccina sourly.

Douglas pointed down the hole. A cramped spiral metal staircase led down to a sub-basement level. "Follow me!"

"Where to?" bawled the colonel. "China?"

"I'm not going!" declared Miss Dalrymple, folding her arms in front of her.

But by that time, Douglas had already bounded eagerly downstairs, and was shouting encouragement up to his group. They looked at each other uneasily. They were hopelessly lost down here, and Douglas was their only guide. They had no choice but to stay with him. One by one, they eased their way gingerly down the stairs, aided by the colonel at the top, and Douglas at the bottom. Finally, they stood panting in the sub-basement.

"Okay," gasped Mr. Buckingham. "This better be good. Where is it?"

"It's here!" Douglas replied. "All around us!" He motioned around the room to where hundreds of wires, cables, and conduit pipes converged on circuit boxes and switches.

The colonel was mystified. "What — wires? Big deal!"

"Not just wires!" Douglas exclaimed. "If we think

of the building as a human being, this is the heart!
These wires are arteries, veins, and capillaries, bring-
ing life-giving blood to all the vital organs!"

Mrs. Dupuis took her husband's arm and headed
back up the spiral staricase. "Come along, Reginald!
We're leaving, with or without our so-called guide!"

"This is it! The brain center! The absolute vortex
of power! Look at these switches! They control everything — the gym lights, the scoreboard — " He began to flick switches on and off at random.

Commando was leading his tour group to their
seats for the basketball game when the lights went
out.

A nervous murmur rose from the sell-out crowd
of alumni, teachers, students, parents, and neigh-
borhood people. Seconds later, the lights came on
again, but power was cut to the scoreboard. Then
the scoreboard came back on, but a murmur from
the crowd out in the front reception area indicated
that *they* were in the dark.

One of the gentlemen from Commando's group
turned to him worriedly. "What's going on?"

"Oh — it's just a test of the electricity," Commando replied with a strange smile. But he knew it
was Doug.

Now the lights were going on and off at random,
playing over the spectators' faces like a flickering
camp fire. Mr. Bell, the custodian, hurried out of the
gym to investigate the problem.

Down on the floor with the Thaddeus G. Little
cheerleaders stood the Richardsons, all anxiety, waiting. Commando checked the crowd. Dave, Yolanda,
Gerald, Anita, and Ric all sat with their groups. There

was no question who the Richardsons were looking for. Doug had taken five innocent people on a ten-minute building tour, and landed them somewhere between the sports building and the earth's core. And wherever he was, he now had control of the lights.

Commando fought down an insane desire to stand up and cheer. Who wanted to watch Kahlil, anyway? Crazy Doug was single-handedly holding up the basketball game.

Douglas scrambled up the metal stairs after his departing tour. "Come back! I'm not finished yet!"

"You are as far as I'm concerned!" snapped Miss Dalrymple.

"Take us to the gym at once!" ordered the colonel.

Douglas looked at him sadly. "You didn't like it."

Colonel Dupuis blew up. "Of *course* I didn't like it! *Nobody* liked it! I'm sixty-seven years old, and this is the stupidest thing that's ever happened to me! Now take us to the game, or we'll go ourselves!"

"You *do* know the way out?" added Mrs. Dupuis.

"Of course," said Douglas. He began to lead them through the labyrinth of corridors. "When we get to the trash compactor, we'll know how to find the furnace room. And once we're there, we can find the air conditioning, which is right by the stairs. So, you see, everything is under con — " He turned a corner and came face to face with a blank wall.

"We're lost!" roared little Mr. Buckingham.

Douglas looked puzzled. "Hmmm."

From above, a roaring cheer could be heard. There was the faint sound of a whistle, then running feet, and the bouncing of a basketball.

"We're missing the game!" exclaimed Mr. Cuccina in a rage.

"Don't worry." Douglas looked around like a scout following a trail. "I've got my bearings again." He pointed. "We go this way."

"That's where we just came from!" exploded Colonel Dupuis.

"This way looks right," said his wife, heading down a blind corridor.

The others trailed after her. Douglas had no choice but to follow.

Mr. Bell descended the metal spiral staircase into the electrical control room. It was empty. Funny — he could have sworn that someone had been playing with the switches.

He did a swift check of all the panel boxes and made sure the circuit breakers were operational. He could hear the sounds of the basketball game directly overhead. Well, if they were playing, then obviously they weren't in the dark. He looked at the switches again and shrugged. It must have been just one of those weird electrical malfunctions.

He climbed up out of the sub-basement, and expertly navigated the corridors. As he closed the furnace room door, he paused. With all the spectators in the building, it might be a good idea to secure this area, he decided. He produced a large ring with many keys on it, found the right one, and locked the door. Then he ran upstairs to catch the rest of the first basketball game to be played in his fabulous new building.

*   *   *

By halftime in the basketball game, anger had given way to panic in the basement. The group had wandered in circles for the last half hour, and even Douglas was out of ideas. Mrs. Dupuis was in tears, being comforted by her irate husband, and everyone was at the point of exhaustion.

"I'm going to sue the school board!" promised Mr. Cuccina.

"And to think that I drove all the way from Baltimore for *this*!" said Miss Dalrymple furiously. "To be trapped in a dungeon by a mad kid!"

"At least you won't have to drive back to Baltimore!" snapped Mr. Buckingham. "I think we're under it! We've walked far enough!"

"I can't go any further!" cried Mrs. Dupuis faintly. "You'll have to leave me behind and send help!" Dramatically, she leaned against the door. It swung open under her weight to reveal —

"The trash compactor!" cried Douglas triumphantly. "I knew we'd find it! Follow me! We'll be at the game in two minutes!"

He led them unerringly down the hall and into the furnace room. "Don't worry. The stairs are right beyond there." He was at the door in two loping strides, and reached out for the handle. It was locked. He tried again, shaking the handle with all his might. It rattled, but would not budge.

"Hmmm."

"Stand aside, boy!" roared Colonel Dupuis. He took a flying run at the door. His shoulder struck the steel plate with a resounding thump, and he bounced off into his wife's arms, cursing.

"Please, sir, don't do that again!" Douglas begged.

"You'll get hurt! I'll find us a way out of this! I promise!" He scanned the room desperately. His eyes fell on a ventilation duct that came out of the furnace and split into a dozen or more paths that disappeared into the walls and ceiling. Eagerly, he attacked the lowest duct. He kicked a three-foot section of tin sheeting off the wall, and crawled in through the hole. On his hands and knees in the cramped space, he turned to his tour group. "Just stay here. I'll crawl out this way and send back help."

Mr. Buckingham was unimpressed. "When you get out, you'd better keep on running! And don't look back, because I'll be behind you with an axe!"

"Hah!" snorted the colonel. "I say we fire up the furnace and roast the little maniac!"

Shuffling and scrambling on the slippery metal surface, Douglas began his journey. It was especially slow going since the duct was sloped fairly steeply, and he would often slide back further than he had climbed forward. But he knew he was going in the right direction, because he could hear the cheering of the crowd and the sounds of the basketball game, and it all seemed to be getting louder.

He felt badly about stranding his alumni group. They were very nice people, even though they didn't appreciate his tour. A Pefkakian would have *loved* it! But Americans preferred glitz over substance, pools over trash compacters.

Now he could see the light at the end of the tunnel. Fifty feet in front of him, he made out an aluminum grating, and beyond it, the bright lights of the gym. Just in time, too. He could feel the all-too-familiar tickle of his postnasal drip nagging at the back of his throat. He scrambled forward at top speed, and looked out. The vent opening was behind one of the baskets, where there were no bleachers, about ten feet up off the floor. He stuck his nose up to the grate and screamed, *"Help!"*

It was halftime, and the cheerleaders were doing their routines to loud music. No one heard him. He grabbed the grating and tried to push it out, but it wouldn't budge. Grimacing with determination, he squeezed his long body around in the duct so that his feet were facing forward. Then he took a deep breath, pulled his knees up to his chest, and let fly with a mighty kick.

The aluminum grating burst out of the wall, sailed through the air and, as though aimed by an evil spirit, dropped into the pack of cheerleaders as they prepared for their grand finale, the human pyramid. It conked Beverly Busby right on the head. A loud scratch shrieked over the P.A. system as the needle was abruptly dragged from the record.

Shocked, Beverly's wild eyes looked up and found the vent just as Douglas' head poked out.

"Excuse me!" bellowed Douglas. "Could somebody please let my tour group out of the furnace room?"

7

Practical Jokers on the Loose

On Monday morning, there was no question about it: The home ec room stank.

"Aw, man, this place is *nasty*!" exclaimed Kahlil, holding his nose.

"Maybe it's the leftover stink from the way you played on Saturday," suggested Carol sarcastically.

Waldo sat down heavily at his desk, groaning. The Minutemen had lost by forty points, and showed no sign of improving — at least, not until a miracle brought Commando back. What a season!

"Who could concentrate on basketball with that nut case coming out of the wall?" shrilled Beverly.

"Come on," said Carol. "You weren't hurt. You're only mad because it was a Twinkie."

"If it wasn't a Twinkie, it wouldn't have happened!" stormed Beverly. "He's a homicidal maniac! He tried to kill me!"

"Yeah, right," called Waldo. "He kicked out that grating, and aimed it at you from ten feet up."

Ms. Castlefield stood at her desk. "All right," she said tiredly. "Someone's left food in one of the drawers, and it's gone bad over the weekend. They can smell it upstairs in Mr. Silverman's office." This got a big cheer. "That will do. Now, check your space, everybody. It's not exactly pleasant working in a room that reeks like a garbage dump."

As the search began, Beverly called her friends together. "Listen," she said in a low voice. "Have any of you guys heard of the Grand Knights of the Exalted Karpoozi?"

"Isn't it the club with the weird sign-up sheet that's all taped together?" asked Carol, checking under a cutlery rack.

"What do they *do*?" Beverly persisted. "I've asked around, and I can't find one person who's a member. I even mentioned it to Mr. Silverman. He's never heard of any Grand Knights."

Waldo shrugged morosely. "Who cares?" With the basketball team losing, he couldn't imagine any other subject capturing a student's interest.

"Well, you've got to admit it's kind of weird," said Beverly. "I mean, I know about every club and social thing that goes on in this school."

Carol laughed. "Why don't you just admit you can't stand the fact that something could be going on, and you aren't even president, or on the executive board, or mixing in somehow?"

"It's not just that," argued Beverly. "I mean, usually the name of a club tells what it is. The Chess Club plays chess; the Event Committee sets up dances and stuff; the Library Club talks about books. What do you do if you're a Knight of the Karpoozi? What's a Karpoozi anyway?"

Kahlil dismissed the whole thing. "They sound like a bunch of morons to me." He punctuated this by slamming a drawer shut.

"Not necessarily," said Beverly. "Maybe they're, like, intellectuals. Or it could be a humor club, and they're going to put out an underground newspaper. The ripped-up sheet could be a joke. You've got to admit humor is something we need in this place, with all the Twinkies around, and the school smelling like a cesspool!"

"Beverly," said the teacher sternly, "this isn't the time to hold court. We have to find whatever's causing that smell."

"Sorry, ma'am."

But naturally, the inspection turned up nothing, as the source of the odor was built into the ceiling.

The smell had even reached the conference room where the Special Discussion Group met at three-thirty.

"Can't they fix it?" demanded Ric.

"But no one knows what it is," explained Julia, smiling.

"A curtain of terror descends on the school," Yolanda intoned dramatically. "Innocent children scatter — bloodcurdling screams echo in the halls. *He* is coming — a fate much worse than death. No one can endure an encounter with — *The Stink!*"

"Have you been watching monster movies again?" Julia asked her.

"Transylvanian Slime Demons," grinned Yolanda.

"I say who cares?" put in Dave. "This school stinks in every other way; it might as well *really* stink."

At four-fifteen, when the group was attempting to file out the front door, Douglas blocked their way. "We need to have a meeting," he informed them.

"We just *had* a meeting," snarled Dave. "I hated it."

"Not the Special Discussion Group," said Douglas. "The Grand Knights of the Exalted Karpoozi."

"Aw, Doug, not that again!" Commando groaned. "Nobody went for your dumb knights, so forget it!"

"But we're in trouble!"

Gerald's normally downcast face snapped to attention. "Trouble?"

"Yeah," Ric chimed in. "How can we be in trouble if we don't even know what you're talking about?"

The group allowed itself to be hustled into the nearby stairwell. Crouched under the flight that led to the second floor, Douglas dropped the bombshell. "Some of you were complaining about the smell in the school." They waited expectantly. "It's us."

"What is?" asked Commando irritably.

"I was going to cook you guys an authentic Pefkakian meal to welcome you into the Grand Knights," Douglas began. He related the story of how the ingredients for the special lunch wound up sealed into the ceiling of the home ec room. "The dry ice is gone, and the food is starting to rot. And it's our fault," he finished.

Commando found his voice first. "Whoa! That's not *our* fault. That's *your* fault. None of us put *any*-

thing in the ceiling of the home ec room."

"But the action can be attributed to the Grand Knights of the Exalted Karpoozi," Douglas argued.

"There are no Grand Knights of the Exalted Karpoozi," Commando refuted. "There's only *you*."

"What was the lunch going to be?" inquired Ric, who was getting hungry.

"Garlic squid with mango and banana."

Dave gagged. "No wonder! *Man*, I'm amazed it doesn't stink *worse!*"

The bag containing her cheerleading outfit slung over her shoulder, Beverly Busby flitted down the front stairs *en route* to her bus home. Suddenly, she stopped dead, frozen by hearing the word that had been on her mind all day — *Karpoozi!* A muffled secret conversation was being held directly beneath the staircase. Beverly strained her ears. This could be about the mysterious Grand Knights!

"Let me get this straight," came a hushed voice. "As Grand Knights, it's our fault the school stinks?"

"Exactly," agreed someone. But then several other voices broke into what sounded like a whispered argument, and it was impossible to make out what any one person was saying.

Excitedly, Beverly tiptoed back up the stairs and ran off. Had she remained another minute, she might have heard Commando announce, "Look, Doug, we're sorry you're up the creek, but you're just not going to convince us this is our fault."

Basketball practice was just letting out when Beverly burst into the gym.

"Guys! Guys!" called Beverly, beckoning to Waldo,

Kahlil, and Carol. "You're never going to believe this! I just found out what those Grand Knight guys do!"

"Flower arranging?" wisecracked Kahlil.

"What's wrong with flower arranging?" demanded Beverly. "My dad happens to be a florist!"

"Sorry," mumbled Kahlil.

"They're a club that plays practical jokes!" grinned Beverly. "And they just cracked a lulu on the whole school! You know the smell in the home ec room? It's a stink bomb set off by the Grand Knights!"

"They told you about it?" asked Carol.

Beverly shook her head. "I just overheard them in the stairwell. I can't even tell you how many kids were in on it. They were whispering, so it was hard to hear. At least four or five, I think."

Waldo was mystified. "Why didn't you just go talk to them?"

Beverly regarded him as though he had a cabbage for a head. "Are you crazy? These guys are *only* the coolest secret club in the whole school! It would be totally geeky to just *walk* up to them!"

Waldo scratched his forehead. "Why?" Beverly had a sense of style that eluded him.

"Because it just would!" she snapped. "How un-cool can you get? Besides," she added, "when the time is right, the Grand Knights of the Exalted Karpoozi will ask me to join up."

Beverly Busby talked to everybody about everything every day, so the news spread like wildfire. The first Commando heard of it came at the eight-forty bell the next morning. As the students entered the school, one sixth-grade girl declared, "Yeccch! I think the smell is getting worse!"

"Yeah," agreed her friend fervently. "Maybe those Grand Knight guys exploded another stink bomb."

Grand Knights? Only the Special Discussion Group knew about the Grand Knights. Unless Doug was shooting off his big mouth for a change!

It happened again at lunch. In the bottleneck caused by Douglas analyzing the applesauce for foreign objects, a group of eighth-grade boys were discussing the home ec room.

". . . and they hid it so well, nobody can find it," the smallest of them was saying. "They say Mr. Stark tore the place apart, but no stink bomb."

"All right, Grand Knights!" cheered his friend. "Hey, what's the holdup here? Is it that tall kid again?" He craned his neck.

"What's so great about a stink bomb?" asked a third boy. "We're the guys who have to smell it!"

"Where's your sense of humor, man?" exclaimed the smaller boy. "These guys laid the ultimate gag on a whole school!" He frowned. "I don't get the Karpoozi part, though."

"Maybe it's part of the joke," suggested his friend. "A joke group should have a joke name."

Commando pushed forward in line.

"Doug!" he whispered urgently. "Did you tell anybody about the squid in the ceiling?"

"Of course not," replied Douglas. "Why?"

Students in the line were regarding them quizzically. The way rumors spread in this school, if anyone overheard them, by tomorrow the Grand Knights would be accused of plotting to overthrow the government!

"I'll tell you later."

Commando couldn't believe it. The home ec

room smelled — *by no fault of his!* — and now a rumor was spreading that the Grand Knights were responsible. And *he* was a Grand Knight. How could he be blamed for something in which he was so blameless? The answer was simple: the same way he'd wound up *off* the basketball team and *on* the Twinkie Squad. And if this little rumor ever trickled up to Mr. Silverman, Commando would *never* get out of the Special Discussion Group.

On the way to Guidance at three-thirty, he eavesdropped on an argument between two seventh-graders outside the home ec room:

"It's obviously a protest against the school board."

"What are you, crazy? Everybody knows it's a comment on how bad the basketball team has been playing. The word is they'll stop the stink when the Minutemen win their first game."

So, at four-fifteen, when the Special Discussion Group meeting ended, the Grand Knights meeting began, in the usual stairwell. Commando started the ball rolling with the bits and pieces of conversation he'd been overhearing all day.

Several of the others had heard the same. "Yeah, these guys were talking about it in the can," offered Ric. "I just figured it was, like, a coincidence. You know — a different Grand Knights."

"What's the big dumb deal?" snorted Dave. "Even if the rumors make it to Silverman, *we're* the only ones who know who the Grand Knights are."

"*Us and* the Richardsons," Commando reminded him. "They could rat us out to Silverman."

"Ooooh, the plot thickens as our heroes descend into a new bloodcurdling level of *terror!*" Yolanda enthused.

"This isn't a movie," Commando said feelingly. "I was kind of hoping to be off the Twinkie Squad before I graduate college." He turned to Douglas. "Okay, genius, you got us into this. Now get us out."

Douglas spoke up. "First, may I say how delighted I am that you're all taking an interest in the Grand Knights — "

"No, you may not!" snarled Dave.

"Get to the point, Doug," prompted Commando.

Dramatically, Douglas unzipped his book bag. There, along with his locked yellow binder, were fifteen bottles of cheap perfume. "Ta-da!"

"Oh, wow!" Anita pulled out a big bottle marked *Essence of French Crocus Musk* and sprayed a giant cloud at her neck.

Douglas snatched the bottle from her hand. "It's not for you. It's for the ventilation system."

"That won't work!" Commando exploded.

"A good smell plus a bad smell equals *no* smell," Douglas reasoned. "It's simple math."

By this time, Anita's perfume had reached Yolanda, who broke into rapturous exclamations of, "*Dah*-ling, it's *mah*-vellous!"

"Hah!" crowed Dave triumphantly. "I got you! You're supposed to be doing horror movies!"

"Buzz off, creep," retorted Yolanda, not from any movie, but as herself.

"Let's do it." The voice was small, but decisive. The group looked with surprise at Gerald Dooley, who was removing several perfume bottles and cramming them into his jacket pockets. This was Gerald, who hardly ever looked up from the floor. "We know we have to do it, so let's do it."

The logic was so sensible that the group wordlessly divided up Douglas' perfume, like soldiers taking up their weapons.

"Onward, Grand Knights — " Douglas began.

"Shut up, Doug," growled Commando. "This is all your fault."

The Grand Knights of the Exalted Karpoozi fanned out to the various ventilation ducts in the school halls to deploy their fragrant ammo.

8

Pick a Card, Any Card

Every year, Thaddeus G. Little Middle School put on a play about the American Revolution. This year's production was called *1776*, and posters throughout the school advertised ticket sales, and encouraged the students to try out for parts.

The auditions began at three-thirty Monday afternoon. Things were just getting underway when the door to the gym opened, and Mr. and Mrs. Richardson marched in with the Special Discussion Group. A murmur went through the assembled students. The Twinkie Squad had arrived.

Instantly, Gerald Dooley tried to sneak back out the door. Julia put an iron grip on his shoulder.

"I promise you, Gerald, you're going to enjoy this. It'll be good for all of us to participate in a large group performance."

"And at least we're in *this* half of the school!" snarled Dave, glaring at Douglas.

The perfuming of the vents had completely back-fired. Instead of covering the squid smell, the sickeningly sweet flower odor of the cheap cologne now hung in the halls like a heavy fog. Together with the rotten food stench from the squid and fruit, it was an unbearable combination.

"Yeah, smooth move, Doug," whispered Commando. "The stink is ten times worse than before!"

"I'm suffering, too," sniffed Douglas. "That substandard perfume has affected my sinuses. I've suffered a relapse of my postnasal drip."

"The worst part is everybody thinks it's another one of our 'famous' Grand Knights practical jokes," said Commando bitterly. "If the news reaches Silverman, that's another useless thing we'll have to take the rap for."

Mr. Torrance, the drama teacher and director of the play, held up his hands for order. "Okay, everybody take a seat, and let's get started."

As the babble of excited voices died down, Beverly Busby sidled up to him. "Sir, why does the Twinkie Squad have to audition?"

"Now, Beverly," replied the director, "you know that everybody has an equal chance to try out."

"I guess," admitted Beverly, who had already wrapped up the role of Martha Washington, since no other girl would dare go up against her. "But it's such a waste of time. Face it — they're not going to get parts. They're going to be stagehands, and gofers, and maybe work the lights."

"Beverly, that will do," Mr. Torrance frowned.

But Beverly knew what she was talking about. Commando mumbled through his lines, then snuck off to spy on basketball practice in the other half of the partitioned gym. Poor Gerald was too shy to squeeze out a single word. When Anita's turn came, she disappeared into the bathroom to fix her hair and never came out. Dave growled out a speech about "stupid Yorktown." Yolanda had just come from a beach movie, and portrayed Betsy Ross as a surfer girl. "Like, this is our totally *radical* new flag, dudes. Hey, man, tasty waves on the Delaware . . ." And Ric never got near the stage. While awaiting his turn, he was climbing the folded bleachers when he lost a handhold, and came crashing down into a bin of volleyballs. He was too dazed to audition.

Mr. Torrance held his head. "Let's get finished with the Special Discussion Group. Okay, you — the tall kid. Read this."

Douglas glanced briefly at the paper, then handed it back to Mr. Torrance, and started on Patrick Henry's famous speech. The forty or so students in the gym fell silent. Commando stepped back around the partition, and stared at Douglas, who stood there, reciting with passion and fire. A moment later, the echoing bounce of the basketball stopped, and Coach Buckley peered into the audition area. Even Waldo, Kahlil, and some of the other players poked their heads out behind their coach.

"I know not what course others may take, but as for me, give me liberty or give me death."

The Richardsons leaped to their feet in a standing ovation. Douglas tried to walk off the stage, but Mr. Torrance stopped him on the stairs.

"You're fantastic!" he raved, pumping the boy's hand in congratulations. "I want you in my play!"

"Well," said Douglas dubiously, "my time is kind of limited. I'm writing a book."

"Mr. Tor-*rance!*" Beverly Busby ran up, in a state of agitation. "Can I talk to you?" She leaned over and whispered in his ear. "You can't make a Twinkie Patrick Henry! You'll ruin the whole play!"

Mr. Torrance looked at Douglas with deep emotion. "You're not going to be Patrick Henry!" he announced in ringing tones. "You're going to be my star!"

"No-o-o-o!" wailed Beverly.

The Richardsons cheered themselves hoarse.

Douglas accepted his copy of the script, with the male lead's lines highlighted in yellow. He glanced at it critically, flipping the pages. "Kind of a dull character, isn't he? Not much personality."

The director stared. "It's George Washington, the father of our country!"

"The father of *your* country," Douglas amended. "I happen to be Pefkakian-born. The father of *my* country is the immortal Ano Pefki."

Mr. Torrance looked completely lost, then assumed a knowing expression. "You must be the ambassador's kid."

It took two days for the perfume odor to fade from the school, but when it did, the smell of rotting squid was still going strong, and nastier than ever.

The sewer expert from the city of Washington took one whiff of the principal's office and announced, "Oh, yeah, it's sewer gas, all right. Worst case in twenty years! Have your pipes been okay?"

"That's why we called *you!*" choked Mr. Silverman from behind a large handkerchief.

The complete sewer gas inspection required that the building be evacuated. The students were overjoyed to comply. The mood in the schoolyard was jubilant.

Waldo was with the usual crowd of basketball players and cheerleaders as Commando approached.

"Remember, we've got the Grand Knights to thank for this," Beverly was saying. "I'll bet they even arranged for the inspector to drop by."

Commando groaned. "Man, this has gone far enough. Look, guys — the Grand Knights are really — "

Beverly cut him off. "Since when do we associate with Twinkies?"

"Come on!" Waldo exploded. "You guys all know Commando's not a real Twinkie!" He waited for a chorus of teammates to chime in their agreement. Instead, he got dead silence.

Commando studied his high-tops. "I'm out of here."

"She didn't mean it!" Waldo exclaimed.

"Take a hike, Rivera," said Kahlil.

"Go hang out with your friend Fairchild," added Beverly.

Staring down an apologetic look from Waldo, Commando strolled off, slowly and casually, careful not to let anyone see how he was burning inside. As far as he was concerned, Beverly could just go on thinking that the Grand Knights were merry pranksters, or the hippest club in school, or the French Foreign Legion for the rest of her snobbish life!

The sewer expert's investigation turned up no trace of sewer gas. After forty-five minutes of unofficial recess, the teachers herded the students to the entrances amid a chorus of boos.

"Three cheers for the Grand Knights!" cried Beverly, and the school hip-hip-hoorayed its way back inside.

Mr. Silverman ran after the sewer expert as he returned to his truck. "Hey, wait! Come back! You can't leave! You've got to help us!"

The man shrugged expansively. "It smells like sewer gas, but it isn't. What can I tell you?"

"Well, what is it, then?"

"I only know sewers," said the man, getting into the cab of his truck. "Your sewers are great. If you want my personal opinion, I think you got a dead animal somewhere in the building." He laughed uproariously. "Counted all the kids lately?"

"But we've searched every inch of this place!" exclaimed the principal in despair.

"Search again. You'd be amazed where mice and rats can end up."

Mr. Silverman made a face. "Thanks."

As rehearsals continued, Douglas began to emerge as the driving force of *1776*. It had taken him exactly one night to memorize not only his own lines, but everyone else's. Only Beverly Busby, still bitter from her bonk on the head with a ventilation grate, was unhappy with Douglas' leadership.

"Rob Norwich would make a good George Washington," she suggested to Mr. Torrance. "Or how about Mark Eisenstein?"

"Now, Beverly," soothed the director. "What's wrong with Douglas? He's a natural!"

She leaned forward confidentially. "But he's supposed to be my *husband*!"

"So?"

She stared at him. "I can't marry a Twinkie!"

At that moment, Douglas breezed in. "Sorry I'm late. I've been working on the script." The star handed Mr. Torrance his copy of *1776*. Under the title was scribbled the words *Revised Version*. To the teacher's puzzled look, Douglas replied, "I penciled in a few minor changes."

The director opened the script and gawked. At least half of the lines were crossed out, with whole new scenes written in the margins in red pen, and even whole new characters. "Bernadette?! Who's Bernadette?"

"A little love interest for General Washington," Douglas explained.

"Love interest?!" howled Beverly. "He's married!"

"It adds a whole new dimension to the character," Douglas reasoned. "He loves Martha, but he can't get Bernadette out of his mind. He's torn. He feels pain. That's drama!"

"I'll play Bernadette!" piped up Anita.

The director ignored them. "Look, Douglas, this is history. There was no Bernadette."

Douglas looked disappointed. "I guess that lets out Albert, then."

"Who?"

"Albert Washington, George's identical twin brother, who fights for the British. I was going to play both roles." Mr. Torrance looked pale. "Well, how about Valley Forge? I think I've really punched up a boring scene."

"I suppose you moved it to Las Vegas!"

"Don't judge it till you've read it," Douglas insisted. "You're going to love this idea." He flipped a few pages ahead. "Picture it. Valley Forge. The place is cold, desolate; the troops are demoralized. They've

just lost Philadelphia. There's hunger, sickness, in-
adequate shelter. General Washington circulates
among the troops, and he says — "

The director's eyes bulged. *"Pick a card, any
card!?"*

"Card tricks?!" cried Beverly.

"Get it?" Douglas crowed. "He's raising the morale
of the soldiers! It's so perfect! It shows that he cares
about the little people!"

"Look, Douglas, forget it," said Mr. Torrance in
bewilderment. "This is ridiculous! There were definitely no card tricks at Valley Forge!"

"There might have been," Douglas argued. "His-
torians often leave out the details that dramatists
consider the most important. Here's the general,
who has big problems, like the birth of a nation, and
the direction of the war. But is he too high and
mighty to bring a little sunshine into the life of even
the lowliest foot soldier? Not George Washington!
It's beautiful!"

"No!" said Mr. Torrance through clenched teeth.
"It's George Washington, not Bob Hope!"

"He's going to be two-dimensional," warned
Douglas.

"I don't care if he's *no*-dimensional!" seethed the
teacher. "Under no circumstances is George Washington going to do card tricks in a play I direct!"

"Now will you think about Mark Eisenstein?"
asked Beverly petulantly.

Mr. Torrance looked at Douglas' earnest face, and
broke into a grin. "I get it." He clapped a friendly
hand on Douglas' shoulder. "What a kidder!" And
he headed for the lighting booth, chortling, "Albert
Washington!"

Beverly turned blazing eyes on Douglas. "If you're going to fool around at rehearsals, we'll never be ready in time for the performance!"

Douglas gazed at her blandly. "Someday Mr. Torrance will realize that just being George Washington doesn't automatically make a character interesting."

Beverly stared at him. "You're serious!"

"Mark my words," was Douglas' dark prediction, "when this play is a flop, I will have been proved right."

"This meeting of the Grand Knights will come to order."

Commando yawned in Douglas' face. "Hurry up, Doug. What's the big idea?"

"It's brilliant! It's brilliant!" cheered Anita.

"He hasn't told us what it is yet," snorted Dave.

"We can't get into the ceiling of the home ec room because the tiles are permanent," said Douglas. "But right next door, the music room has a suspended ceiling."

"So what?" countered Commando. "We'll be in the right place in the wrong room."

"I volunteer!" piped Anita.

"But you won't fit," Commando protested.

"I'm getting fat, aren't I?" Her tone was tragic.

"*We're* not going up there," Douglas interrupted.

"Then who is?" asked Ric.

Douglas beamed. "Willy and Milly."

"Who?"

The door to the deserted music room opened, and in snuck the Grand Knights, Douglas in the lead. In one hand, he carried a powerful stage spotlight that was being used for the play; in the other, a small wire cage containing two gerbils.

"I got the idea when Mr. Poppolini was telling us about how rodents will eat anything. If we release Willy and Milly into the ceiling, the odor will attract them straight to the squid. They'll eat it, and we'll have them back in their cage before anyone even notices they're gone. No squid, no smell."

"How do you know they'll come back when they're done?" asked Commando.

In answer, Douglas produced a coil of string. As Commando held the squirming gerbils, he carefully looped a knot around each furry neck.

Yolanda flattened herself against the wall. "I'll stand guard," she hissed. "There could be enemy agents around the corner."

Douglas stepped up onto a chair and pushed open the suspended ceiling. All at once, a paralyzing blast of squid stink hit the room.

"Oh, man!" gasped Dave.

"At least we know we're in the right place," choked Douglas cheerfully. "The gerbils, please."

His nose buried in his sleeve, Commando handed Willy and Milly up to Douglas, who released them into the ceiling. *"Bon apetit."*

Everyone watched the ceiling, and the bottom half of Douglas. There was a pause, then, "No, you in-competent rodents, you're going the wrong way! Get the squid! The squid!"

"Problems, Doug?" called Commando.

Douglas looked down at him. "I can't see a thing up here. Hand me the light."

The five-thousand-watt spotlight lit up the foot-high world of the ceiling. Willy and Milly were puttering in the dust, as far from the squid as their string leashes would allow them to go. "Why aren't they attracted to the squid?"

"Would *you* be?" asked Commando. "Face it. This is another stupid idea."

"Don't blame me. Blame Mr. Poppolini. His knowledge of animal behavior is severely flawed."

Poking around the small opening, Douglas brushed his cheek against the hot theatrical bulb.

"Yeeeeow!" He lost his grip on the light, kicked over his chair, and grabbed hold of the ceiling frame, dropping the big lamp into Commando's hands.

"Hot!" cried Commando. He bobbled the spot over to Anita, who juggled it over to Gerald, who managed to hold on by a wire.

Douglas jumped to the floor. "That was close." Then he noticed his hands no longer held the two strings.

"Where are Willy and Milly?" demanded Dave.

Douglas pointed at the ceiling. "Up there."

Dave righted the chair, scrambled up onto it, and crammed his head into the opening. *"Willy!"* he bellowed. *"Milly!"*

Commando dragged him down. "Are you nuts?" he hissed. "Do you want Silverman on our necks?"

Dave was purple. "We've got to find them!"

Gerald shrugged expansively. "They could go anywhere in the whole school — ceilings, walls — "

"But there's no food!" cried Dave. "They'll starve!"

"They can always eat the squid," put in Douglas.

Dave was in a rage. "How would you feel if someone twenty times your size trapped you in a strange dark place with no way to get out?"

Commando looked him in the eye. "Why are you getting so worked up about this?"

"Because — " Dave's voice cracked. "Because I can't stand it when bad things happen to furry little animals!" A chorus of guffaws greeted this confession.

Commando laughed the loudest. "*You*? You hate everything, man! Since when do you have this soft spot for gerbils?"

"Shut up!" growled Dave."All of you! Now — are we going to save Willy and Milly, or what?"

Anita spoke up. "Of course we are! Of *course* we are!"

Commando stared at her. "How?"

"They're goners," mourned Anita. "They haven't got a chance."

An insistent scratching sound came from behind them. The Grand Knights wheeled to look at the heating vent on the far wall close to the floor. Two pairs of beady little eyes were staring out through the bars of the grate, for all the world like small furry prison inmates.

"Willy and Milly!" cried Dave. "Quick, somebody bring the cage!" He opened the grill, but the gerbils backed away, timidly. "Aw, c'mon, guys. I was worried about you!" He poked a finger into the vent. "Come on out. Pretty please?" Milly nuzzled up and nipped him. "Ow!"

"Still feel the same about furry animals?" laughed Commando, holding out the cage.

Dave grinned sheepishly. From his pocket he pulled out a small white card and offered it at the mouth of the vent. Instantly, Milly grabbed the card, and both gerbils toppled out of the opening to the floor, chewing with gusto on the small piece of cardboard.

Douglas stared in horror. "That's your Grand Knights membership card!"

"Big deal," sneered Dave. "What's it good for — besides getting us blamed for stuff we didn't even do?"

"Have some respect!" stormed Douglas. He attempted to snatch the card away from Willy and Milly, but succeeded only in frightening them. The gerbils dashed across the room into the shadows. Milly still held Dave's card in her mouth.

"Aaaah!" cried Dave in shock.

"Get them!" ordered Commando.

In the wild chase that followed, nobody noticed the smoke that was beginning to rise from the big spotlight, which was lying on the carpet. When it reached the ceiling smoke detector, the fire alarm wailed throughout the school.

Commando threw his hands up. "What next, huh?"

Willy and Milly squeezed under the door and bolted into the hall.

9

Dr. Footsie

"*May I have your attention, please,*" came the voice over the P.A. system the next morning. "*This is Mr. Poppolini. Someone played a very cruel joke yesterday afternoon. If anyone knows who let Willy and Milly out of their cage and then pulled the fire alarm, please come to see me in the science room. The gerbils could very easily have been trampled as we evacuated the building. As it was, it took over four hours to find Willy and Milly and get them back in their cage. Oh yes, special thanks to Beverly Busby, who got Milly out of the girls' change room.*"

In first-period home ec class, Beverly got a standing ovation. The home ec room had been shut down, so Ms. Castlefield now conducted her lessons in the kitchen of the cafeteria.

"That's not all," Beverly whispered to Carol, Waldo, and Kahlil. "Look what Milly had in her mouth!" From her pocket she pulled out a small tattered white card.

" 'The Grand Knights of the Exalted Karp'?" read Kahlil in perplexity.

"It's Karpoozi, stupid! The end got chewed off. It's a Grand Knight's membership card!"

"Whose is it?" asked Carol.

"That part's gone, too," admitted Beverly.

"So what's so great about it?" asked Waldo.

Beverly looked at him pityingly. "It proves that the Grand Knights were behind this thing!"

"Are you going to tell Mr. Poppolini?" asked Carol.

"Of course not! This was almost as funny as the stink bomb. You should have seen Mr. Poppolini crawling around the girls' change room. I almost cracked up! And I need a good laugh, with the way the play's been going lately!"

As rehearsals for *1776* progressed, General Washington was beginning to change. First, there were long stony pauses to indicate the general's inner pain. Then Douglas switched to a jovial George Washington, complete with belly laughs, back-slapping, and even a few one-liners.

"How many British does it take to load a cannon?"

"That isn't in the script!" shrieked Mr. Torrance.

"Five!" chuckled General Washington. "One to hold the ball — "

"Mr. Torrance, he's doing it again!" wailed Beverly.

Douglas looked disappointed. "Don't you want to hear what the other four do?"

"No!"

Douglas reached into his pocket and produced a deck of cards. "Well, how about this, then? A perfectly normal two of spades — but look — "

The director blew his stack. "Stop! Stop it! Get those cards off my stage!"

"How about this?" Commando suggested. "We put my skateboard right inside the door, so when he steps on it, he rolls towards the living room. Now, we've got one of those inflatable wading pools from when I was a kid. If we fill it with water, he'll end up right in it!"

Commando and Douglas were walking along G Street, contemplating tonight's booby trap.

"Won't he just fall down when he gets one foot on the skateboard?" asked Douglas.

"Nah. Dad's got great balance. He used to be a roller champion."

Douglas shook his head. "It's still too risky," he declared. "If he sprains his right wrist, he won't be able to write the CPA exam. How's this? He comes home; he's expecting a trap. But there's nothing. All evening, he's going crazy, waiting for the axe to fall."

"What's so great about that?" asked Commando. "Nothing happens."

"It's psychological warfare," Douglas explained. "Much worse than a skateboard and a wading pool."

"We could take all the furniture and move it up-stairs," mused Commando. "That way, when he comes home and sees the place cleaned out, he'll think we've been robbed."

Douglas shook his head. "Lifting heavy objects aggravates my postnasal drip."

They ran up the stairs, and Commando unlocked the door.

"Hey, Comm," came Mr. Rivera's voice.

"It's my dad!" hissed Commando. "Watch yourself! There's a booby trap here somewhere!"

Mr. Rivera stepped out of the kitchen. "Things were slow at the office, so I took the afternoon off. Oh, hi, Douglas. How's it going?"

"Fine, sir," said Douglas warily, looking around.

"You guys thirsty?" asked Mr. Rivera. "I just made some iced tea."

Douglas and Commando were still scouting around for traps, but Mr. Rivera just cleared a spot for them at the kitchen table, which was covered with textbooks, notes, and computer printouts.

"Maybe he's using psychological warfare," whispered Douglas. "He could have thought of it first."

Mr. Rivera poured three tall glasses from a pitcher of iced tea, and they all sat down.

"It's the iced tea!" whispered Commando triumphantly. "Let *him* drink first!" They sat expectantly.

"Aren't you going to try it?" asked Mr. Rivera. To set an example, he took a large gulp from his own glass. "Ahhh! Studying can be thirsty work."

Tentatively, as though the glass were about to explode, Commando picked it up and sniffed. The aroma was definitely tea. He tasted it. Tea. It wasn't a trap. Douglas tasted his and seemed to agree.

"Great tea, Dad." Commando reached for the sugar bowl, scooped three heaping spoonfuls into both his drink and Douglas', and stirred. The two boys drank deeply.

And choked.

Commando spat a stream across the table, into his father's notes. Douglas made it to the sink.

"*Salt!*" rasped Commando.

Mr. Rivera was on his feet, jumping up and down, clapping, and cheering his practical joke. "I *nuked* you guys! I knew you'd do that! You'd add sugar to maple syrup!"

Douglas was draped over the counter, head in the sink, drinking directly from the tap.

Commando grabbed the pitcher of tea and took a mighty gulp. "Salt in the sugar bowl!" he croaked. "You have a sick mind!"

"Utterly deranged!" agreed Douglas.

"Thanks," beamed Mr. Rivera. "I knew you'd like it."

Commando pulled a napkin from the holder and began to dab at his father's splashed notes. "Sorry about the mess, Dad. How's the studying coming?"

His father shrugged miserably. "You know, if you stare at numbers long enough, they move. Yesterday I was following this '8' around the page. I'm pretty sure I'm losing my mind."

Douglas clucked sympathetically. "After you pass the test, you should consider taking a vacation in Pefkakia."

The first scene of the rehearsal was Valley Forge. The curtain rose on George Washington's tent. A poster was tacked to the side. It read:

> *Don't be scared, don't be skittish,*
> *Just go out and cream the British.*

By this time, there was no question of who to go to for an explanation. "It's a catch phrase," said Douglas. "Like a jingle that's always running around in your head. The troops can sing it out as they march into battle."

"Mark Eisenstein's been complaining that he's got

nothing to do with his afternoons," Beverly Busby suggested hopefully.

"Look, it's too late to start from scratch with a new star," said Mr. Torrance angrily. "Believe me, if it wasn't, Fairchild would be out on his fanny!"

By the end of the week, Mr. Torrance, at his wits' end, called in the Richardsons. Martin and Julia passed the director's comments on to Douglas at the Friday meeting of the Special Discussion Group.

Douglas was ready for them. "Mr. Torrance isn't a very good director. That's why I have to take it on myself to jazz up this Washington character."

The Richardsons' famous double smile wavered in stereo. "Mr. Torrance was sort of hoping you would — you know — cut it out," Martin managed.

Ric was making giant circles in the air with his head. "Like — you said you wanted us to get involved in this play." The twirling stopped. "Well, Douglas is more involved than anybody."

"Yeah," said Yolanda. "Every year you make us try out, and they always make us stagehands, curtain-pullers, and stuff. This year one of us got to be George Washington. So don't hassle it."

"What movie is that from?" asked Commando.

Yolanda looked completely blank.

"Well, how about the rest of us?" Julia beamed. "Armando, are you enjoying your part in the play?"

"What part?" mumbled Commando. "I get coffee for Torrance. I could do that at Ralph's diner for three-fifty an hour."

"You can't look at it that way," smiled Julia. "A play requires a lot of different kinds of work, and we each contribute in our own way. Yolanda works on scenery. And Ric is a British soldier."

"They won't let me be that anymore," said Ric.

"Why not?"

"I stabbed myself with a bayonet."

Dave snickered loudly. "I remember that!" he guffawed. "It was great!"

An hour later, the seven members of the Special Discussion Group were packed into three phone booths outside the Thaddeus G. Little office, hiding. A new plan was underway.

R-r-r-ring!

Commando looked shocked. "Who knows we're in here?"

Dave reached up from a squat and snatched down the receiver. "Hello? . . . oh, yeah." He handed the phone to Commando. "It's for you."

Furious, Commando grabbed it. "Who *is* this?"

"Is he gone yet?" came Douglas' voice.

"You paid a quarter to ask me that?"

"I can't see," Douglas complained. "Ric's blocking my view."

"Silverman's just putting his coat on," whispered Commando. "He'll be gone in a second. Sit tight, and keep Ric still. He's rocking your booth."

The principal switched off the office lights and headed out of the building to the parking lot.

The seven emerged from hiding.

"What was going on?" Anita demanded. "I tried calling, but the line was busy!"

Commando rolled his eyes. "Okay, Doug, what's the game plan?"

Douglas indicated the toolbox Gerald hugged to his chest. "We're going to drill holes in Mr. Silverman's floor, and drop foot powder on the squid."

"Brilliant!" breathed Anita.

"Aw, come on!" complained Commando. "You said you had a real idea!"

"This *is* a real idea," Douglas protested. "We've attacked it from below. Now we have to attack it from above. This office is directly above."

The office was the second smelliest room in the school. (Home ec was number one.) Douglas handed out handkerchiefs to be worn bandito-style, so the group looked more like train robbers than Grand Knights.

Yolanda pulled the principal's big swivel chair away from his desk, and Commando and Ric rolled back the dull beige rug. Douglas stood poised, looking with a gold prospector's eye over the hardwood floor.

"Hurry up!" prompted Dave. "I want to go visit Willy and Milly."

"Quiet, please," murmured Douglas. "I'm trying to remember exactly where — I — put it." As he spoke, he moved to the center of the cleared area and pointed to a spot on the floor. "The drill, please."

Gerald handed him a manual drill from the tool-box. Kneeling, Douglas worked the device, its quarter-inch bit boring through the floorboards.

"That's it!" moaned Commando. "I can't believe we're doing this! It's stupid! It's vandalism! It's — "

And then the smell hit. It was twenty times worse than in the music room. The handkerchiefs were useless here. The seven could almost feel the presence of rotten garlic squid with mango and banana enveloping them in its rancid clutches.

"Did anyone ever die from a stink?" gasped Ric, flattening himself against the far wall.

But Douglas looked pleased. "We must be close." He lay flat on his face, shining a flashlight through the hole and peering in with one squinting eye. "I can see the corner of the bag. One more opening right — here!" He punched another quarter-inch hole and peered down with the flashlight. "Bulls-eye! We're right over it!"

"Ready for the foot powder?" Yolanda held out a huge box marked *Dr. Footsie, endorsed by champion marathon runner Gavin Gunhold, Giant Economy Size.*

"Why foot powder?" asked Commando.

Douglas shrugged. "If it can deodorize Gavin Gunhold's feet after a twenty-six-mile run, squid should be no problem." Painstakingly, he used the drill bit to puncture a tiny hole in the top of the box. Then, very carefully, he tilted the Dr. Footsie.

Fooomp!

The top of the box came off, and six pounds of foot powder avalanched out, sending up a dust cloud that reached the ceiling. The others coughed and waved their arms to clear the air in front of them, but Douglas began honking like a Canada goose, his postnasal drip in full swing.

Suddenly they heard footsteps in the outer office, and Mr. Silverman's voice mused, "Now, where did I leave those attendance records?"

Commando clamped his hand firmly over Douglas' nose and mouth. Ric slammed the rug back down, sending clouds of foot powder far and wide, and began jumping up and down on the lump formed by the mountain underneath.

"The toilet!" rasped Commando. "Flush it down the toilet!"

Ric was wide-eyed. "The *carpet?*"

"No, stupid! The foot powder!"

To set an example, Gerald flung the carpet back up, grabbed a handful of Dr. Footsie, and ran to the small private bathroom. The others did the same.

The footsteps in the hall got closer.

"Faster!" rasped Commando. He threw the rug back into place, smoothed it down, and packed himself along with the others into the tiny washroom.

They waited, struggling for standing room, scarcely daring to breathe. Gerald pulled the door shut, making the squeeze even tighter. Yolanda's elbow was in his face. Douglas was pressed into a corner, wheezing into the tiles. Ric stood on the toilet seat, his head against the ceiling. Dave and Anita were huddled under the sink. All were white with foot powder, and frozen with fear. Had they cleaned up enough?

"Ah, here they are," came the principal's voice, still outside. There were more footsteps, receding this time, and then — nothing.

"He didn't even come in!" exclaimed Yolanda in outrage. "After all our hard work!"

"Our troubles are over!" grinned Ric. As he let himself down from the toilet seat, he accidentally hit the flusher. This led to a major discovery: Dr. Footsie blocks toilets.

"Aw, no!" moaned Commando. "No! No! No! What else could go wrong today?" The overflow hit the floor. Commando grabbed the handy plunger and began pumping.

Douglas sniffled experimentally. "Ah! My nasal passages are returning to normal."

"Whoop-de-do," said Commando and kept on pumping.

10

The Broom Closet

When Commando arrived at school on Monday morning, he found a map of the building taped to his locker, marked with directions to an obscure broom closet tucked away at the far end of the school. An attached note informed him that he had to see Mr. Silverman there.

Commando laughed out loud. Now that the smell was coming up through the two quarter-inch drill holes under the rug, the principal's office had become unbearable. Apparently, Dr. Footsie foot powder was a bust. Maybe Gavin Gunhold's marathon feet could be sweetened by it, but rotting Pefkakian food was another story.

The door was marked *357–Storage*, but a hand-lettered sign on a shirt cardboard read: *OFFICE*.

Commando knocked, and entered.

"Ah, Armando. Good morning."

Mr. Silverman's desk extended the entire width of

the tiny room. The principal must have had to climb over it to get to his swivel chair, which was jammed into a forest of upside-down mops and brooms.

"Good morning, sir." Commando was surprised to find Coach Buckley there as well.

"How ya doin', champ?" Buckley greeted him.

"Well, Armando, you've been taking your punishment very well," observed Mr. Silverman.

Commando looked back at him blandly. He noted that the rag portion of an enormous push mop was poised above the principal's head, as though about to eat him.

"There's been no fighting, either," Mr. Silverman went on. "I'm impressed. I think you should be rewarded for this good behavior. All I want from you is a five-hundred-word essay admitting that it was wrong to attack the Fairchild boy, and you'll be out of the Special Discussion Group and back on the Minutemen. How does that sound?"

Commando's heart leaped. Here it was — a chance to be back on the team, to be done with the Twinkie Squad, or the Grand Knights, or whoever they were! Never to have to tell Dad about these last few weeks! A chance to be a normal person again, with normal friends! All he had to do was —

"I didn't attack anybody."

"Now we've been through this before," said Mr. Silverman warningly.

"That doesn't change the truth," replied Commando. "Doug Fairchild got hit with a basketball."

"I'm giving you a chance to put all this behind you," said Mr. Silverman in growing annoyance.

"I think maybe you just don't want to lose any more basketball games," said Commando quietly.

He cast a crooked smile at the coach. "Am I that good, or is Kahlil that bad?"

Coach Buckley said nothing.

Mr. Silverman leaped to his feet, upsetting a large metal pail that bounced off his desktop and clattered to the floor. "All right! Have it your way! But I say you were caught red-handed!"

Commando bit his tongue. Now was the perfect time to point out that the person he was supposed to have beaten up had been just about his only friend since all this had started.

Aloud, he said, "I guess if the Minutemen were having a good season, I'd be on the Twinkie Squad for life."

Mr. Silverman was about to blow his stack, so Coach Buckley stepped in. "Okay, I'll talk to him." He led Commando outside and turned on him angily. "What's the matter with you, Rivera? Don't you *want* to play ball?"

Commando shook his head. "Not if I have to admit that I did something I didn't do."

"Look," said the coach in exasperation, "write the essay. I'll help you. We'll say fighting is bad, and nobody should do it, and we'll never actually admit you popped Fairchild. Who's going to read it?"

Commando pointed at the "office" door. "He will. Every word."

Buckley looked at him imploringly. "We *need* you, Rivera. We're getting shelled worse every game! Parents have been complaining!"

Commando shook his head. "I'm sorry. I loved being on the team, and you've always been great to me, Coach. But I can't let Silverman win this. He *dissed* me! And I lost a lot more than a spot on the team. All Waldo misses is twenty passes a game, not me. Team members have been getting on my case — even some cheerleaders who don't want to be seen with a Twinkie." He pointed at the door again. "I can't let him win — not for the team, not for *anything!*"

Buckley nodded sadly. "You really *didn't* hit him, did you?"

"What do you think?"

"You're the straightest kid who ever played for me," the coach admitted. "You stick to your guns, and never mind the team. For what it's worth, you've got my respect for good and always."

Commando smiled. "It's worth a lot, Coach. Thanks."

The two shook hands and went their separate ways.

At lunch, Commando was making his way to the cafeteria when Waldo Turcott exploded onto the scene, over the moon with happiness.

"Welcome back, Mr. Point Guard!" He picked up the smaller boy and twirled him around, spiraling through the cafeteria door and into the food line. "The Turcott-Rivera scoring machine is *back in business!*"

"I turned him down," said Commando.

It took a few seconds for the words to register on Waldo. "We're going to roll over the competition! Kick some serious butt! With you shakin' and bakin', and me owning the paint — you *what?*" He dropped Commando like a hot potato. *"Why?"*

"I had my reasons," said Commando simply.

Waldo looked up at the ceiling and roared his

outrage. "You can't do this to me! I just told Kahlil what I thought of him, because I heard you were coming back! I told him my grandmother plays better point guard in her motorized wheelchair!"

"You lost by forty points last game," Commando reasoned. "I'm better than Kahlil, but I don't think it's forty points' worth."

"It *is*!" bellowed Waldo, shaking Commando like a rag doll. "First of all, *they'd* score less because *you* play defense! Then *I'd* score twenty more because you'd give me the ball! And *you'd* pump in twenty from outside — compared with Kahlil going 0 for 35!" He shook harder. "Go back to Silverman! Tell him you changed your mind! Tell him the stink in the school messed up your head, and you didn't know what you were saying! Tell him anything! Just don't do this to me!"

"Hey!" There was a tug at Waldo's shirt. Waldo released Commando and looked around. But since he was looking at his own eye level, he failed to see little Gerald Dooley, fists clenched, ready for war. "Lay off Commando!" Gerald demanded.

Waldo stared down at him in total amazement. "What?"

"Lay off Commando," Gerald repeated fiercely, "or you'll be sorry!"

"Look, Gerald," Commando managed, "it's okay. We're just having a discussion."

The slight ten-year-old stood his ground. Beyond Gerald, Ric Ewchuk had gotten up from his table and was scrambling over, eyes intent on Waldo. A few feet behind him strode Yolanda, her face calm, but tough as nails.

Commando suppressed an insane desire to giggle. "It's okay, Ric. No problem, Yolanda," he called out. "Really, we're just hanging out."

Reluctantly, Gerald and Ric returned to their tables. So did Yolanda, but not before giving Waldo a look of pure danger. "Go ahead," she said. "Make my day."

Waldo walked away without another word, and Commando began selecting his lunch. He was at the cashier when he realized what had just happened. *The Twinkie Squad was starting to stick together!* Three Twinkies, who never thought about anything except their own weird problems, had just rushed like the cavalry to rescue him! Now what had brought *that* on?

Beverly Busby had noticed the incident as well and had advice for Waldo as he sat down. "Stay away from the Twinkies. They're crazy. One of them could have a grenade or something."

Carol laughed right in her face. "You know, you've got to do something about your obsession with the Twinkies. Okay, they're a little weird, but that doesn't automatically mean they're armed to the teeth."

"Go ahead and laugh!" challenged Beverly. "That Ric guy is wired! And you can all see how Crazy Fairchild is wrecking *1776.*"

"There's a big difference between card tricks and a grenade," Carol pointed out. "And Ric can't help the way he is. The guy's hyperactive."

"You mean hyperstupid," amended Beverly. "Hey, did you guys hear the latest? Silverman's out of his office — he's working in some broom closet. The Grand Knights set off another stink bomb. Sabotaged his toilet, too!"

Carol snorted. "This is just like you, Bev. Poor

Fairchild messes up a bit during rehearsal, and he's public enemy number one; but when the Grand Knights wreck the whole school, they're the coolest club around!"

Beverly stared at her. "How can you compare the Grand Knights to a Twinkie? Bite your tongue!"

Waldo was concentrating on Kahlil, who was picking peas out of a bowl of vegetable soup and discarding them on his napkin. "Yo, Kahlil, man, can I treat you to some dessert?"

Kahlil was surly. He turned to Carol. "Tell Turcott that if I play like his grandmother, *he* plays like my *great*-grandmother, who's dead!"

"That's it?" hooted Carol. "You had all morning to think up a return insult, and that's the best you can do?"

"Hey, man," retorted Kahlil, "I let my game do the talking."

"Then you don't say much," retorted Carol evenly.

With the play scheduled for Friday night, the last week of rehearsals became more and more intense. If Mr. Torrance had been nervous before, he was now a total wreck, vibrating like a guitar string. Commando spent whole practices going back and forth to the coffee machine for the director. And despite warnings, threats, and begging and pleading, Douglas continued to experiment, searching for the true character of the first president.

On Tuesday, he played General Washington with a slight limp. As the play wore on, the limp grew more pronounced until, by Yorktown, he was dragging his leg and groaning loudly.

On Wednesday, he played up General Washington

as a "nice guy" by delivering a long speech forgiving Benedict Arnold for his "little peccadillo."

The play had been moved to the high school auditorium because of the ongoing smell problem at Thaddeus G. Little. All sets were loaded onto a bus and taken over to the new site.

"What a hassle!" grunted Carol, lugging a box of swords down G Street. "What do you think of your precious Grand Knights now?"

"What are you — crazy? This is *way* better!" exclaimed Beverly. "Instead of a beat-up old gym, we'll be in a real auditorium!"

Dress rehearsal was the time for weeks of effort to come together. The set painters got their first look at their work onstage. The actors tried on their costumes. Painted plywood scenery whizzed by in all directions. Props were handed from actors to stagehands to actors again. Scripts fluttered. Voices recited lines. Commando got coffee for the director.

Soon all was in readiness and the dress rehearsal could begin. The first scene of *1776* took place at the home of George Washington, then a successful Virginia planter. Some local country squires come by to tell of the passage of the Stamp Act. The effect of the eighteenth-century costumes and elaborately painted sets was impressive, and Beverly Busby was the perfect Martha Washington, bustling around in her apron, cap, and calico gown.

She called to her husband, "Oh George, you have visitors."

And then Douglas Fairchild entered from stage left, dressed head to toe in a white bunny suit, complete with long pink ears and powder-puff tail.

"Ahhhh!" shrieked Martha Washington.

Mr. Torrance sprayed coffee all over Commando. *"Fairchild, you lunatic!"* he choked. "What do you think you're doing?"

Douglas laughed. "Oh, this. Don't worry, sir. I won't be wearing it tomorrow night, of course."

"Why are you wearing it *now*?"

"Well, you see," Douglas explained, "George Washington is such an important historical character that my fellow actors are intimidated by me, which makes the general seem aloof and snobbish. But tomorrow night, they'll be able to picture me the way I am today. And it's impossible to be intimidated by a bunny, even if he's the father of your country. So he'll appear more human."

Beverly picked up a long-handled warming pan and swung it at Douglas, who hopped out of the way just in time.

"Rivera!" barked the director. "Disarm Beverly. And be careful with that thing! It's an antique!" He turned on Douglas. "If you're not in your costume in two seconds, the cast party tomorrow will be serving rabbit stew!"

Douglas' ears sagged dejectedly. "Well, could I show you some card tricks? I've got a couple that are really dignified — "

"Get off my stage!"

11

The British Are Coming

"You know, Admiral Strickland's gala is called for nine," commented Ambassador Anton Fairchild as his limo whispered down G Street.

"We'll be late, that's all," replied his wife. "Douglas would be heartbroken if we missed his play."

"He begged us not to come," Ambassador Fairchild pointed out. "He said — and I quote — 'It would be more interesting to watch prunes stew.' "

She smiled. "Oh — you know Douglas."

"No, I don't," he said seriously. "I *never* did. How about all that gibberish about being denied the creative freedom to three-dimensionalize his character. I went to college — what is he talking about?"

"Everyone else is putting on a cute little school play, and Douglas wants it to be perfect. He won't even talk about the play, or tell me what part he has. He's keeping it all a surprise."

"He's probably playing a tree," quipped the ambassador, "and driving everybody crazy with his method acting." He sighed. "That boy's my own son, and he may as well be from Mars for all that I understand him."

His wife chuckled. "Well, he *is* from Pefkakia."

The famous couple laughed all the way to Washington High.

The auditorium was resplendent with red, white, and blue. The stage was framed with streamers and bunting, and revolutionary flags hung from the walls. The stagehands were passing out programs, and seating the many students, parents, and brothers and sisters in attendance.

Commando was escorting Beverly Busby's parents to VIP seats when he spied his father being led in by Gerald Dooley. He ran over.

"Hey, Dad, what are you doing here?"

"The school sent notices to all the parents," said Mr. Rivera. "Why didn't you tell me you were in the play?"

Commando made a mental note to check the mail more carefully. "Because I'm not. I do this and get coffee for the director. That's my job."

Mr. Rivera shrugged. "You're part of it." He watched as Gerald silently slunk away from them. "Weird kid. Doesn't say too much."

"He's only ten. He got bumped up a year. I hear his I.Q. is 160." Commando grinned. "Hey, I thought you had a class tonight."

"I got some guy to take notes for me," Mr. Rivera replied. "I figure if you can handle basketball practice *and* rehearsal, the least I can do is come and see the play." He smiled. "For my money, Comm, you're the best usher here."

Commando laughed uncomfortably. Mention of basketball reminded him of all the things he hadn't been telling his father lately. "Come on, Dad. As long as you're here, you may as well sit in the front row." He took his father to the best seat in the house, across the aisle from the Busbys. "I should warn you — this play might be kind of interesting. Keep you eye on Doug. He's George Washington."

"Why?"

"Well, for starters," replied Commando, "he did the dress rehearsal in a rabbit suit." He turned to the door. "More customers. I've got to get back to work."

Commando scrambled to take his place as an usher. He stood waiting as other pages walked off with their guests. And then it was his turn. There in the doorway stood Ambassador and Mrs. Anton Fairchild. Even though he now knew them, it was still a thrill to see the two famous faces in person. "Hey, Mr. and Mrs. Fairchild. Remember me? Commando."

The ambassador blinked. "I've been meaning to talk to you. How did you know I'd be going to Helsinki? The President only told me today."

Commando flushed with pleasure. "I watch *Political Diary* every day." He led the ambassador and his wife to the two front-row seats right beside David Rivera. Bursting with excitement, he drew himself up to his full height of five feet one inch, and performed the introduction. "Ambassador and Mrs. Fairchild, this is my father, David Rivera."

The three exchanged greetings and handshakes.

Commando handed Douglas' parents a mimeographed program. "Well, enjoy the play, sir — ma'am. Oh — when you're in Finland, the pressure's going to be on for you to give in on the Polar Icecap treaty. Don't budge."

"You've got it," said the ambassador, nodding decisively.

Mr. Rivera smiled at the Fairchilds. "You'll have to excuse Comm. He's the only eleven-year-old politics cheerleader in America."

"He seems like a fine young man," said the ambassador and turned his attention to his program. "Douglas Fairchild — *George Washington?*" He looked at his wife. "This is the boring role he's been complaining about? *George Washington?* The lead?"

"Anton, don't be so cynical," his wife chided. "You can't fool me. I see your smile. I'm proud of him, too."

Backstage was bedlam as the cast and crew scurried around making last-minute adjustments on clothing, scenery, and lights. Mr. Richardson peeked through the curtain. "They're all seated," he announced.

Mr. Torrance was circulating among his actors, checking details and calming last-minute jitters. "Okay," he called. "Dim the houselights."

Gerald pulled the switch, and the house went dark.

Mr. Torrance was pink with anticipation. "This is it, people!" In a last-minute pep talk, he urged his actors to "let go" onstage, and breathe life into their characters.

All except one. The director had special instructions for Douglas, and he delivered them right before curtain time. "Fairchild," he said, "I've been a teacher for twenty-two years, and so far I've never killed a student. Don't make me break my perfect record."

And before Douglas could reply, Mr. Torrance signaled Gerald to raise the curtain.

The Fairchilds sat riveted to their seats, watching their son's performance. Douglas was magnificent. In his authentic uniform, wig, and hat, he *became* George Washington. His bearing was proud and military, and he spoke with the authority of a man at the helm of the birth of a nation. Even his fellow actors were impressed, performing their lines in awed respect. And if his wife, Martha, seemed to look at him with loathing, it went unnoticed by most people.

Mrs. Fairchild took her husband's hand. "Well, Anton," she whispered. "What do you think of your son now?"

The ambassador was glowing with pride. "He's really talented!"

Mr. Rivera leaned over to Mrs. Fairchild seated beside him. "Congratulations. He's terrific."

In the third row sat Mr. Silverman, spellbound by Douglas' performance. He beamed at the Richardsons.

"Julia — Martin — fine work."

Commando watched from the wings. Unbelievable as it seemed, Doug was pulling it off. After three weeks of torturing the cast and crew with bizarre new ways to portray George Washington, here he was, not just playing it straight, but putting on an Academy Award performance! What a guy!

He glanced at Mr. Torrance, who was mouthing

the lines along with his actors, and providing encouragement and support. The director was tense, but jubilant. Even in his nervousness, he had to realize what a big hit *1776* was shaping up to be.

Mr. Torrance did not relax until the play was about halfway through. Philadelphia had just fallen. General Washington declared, "We will regroup at Valley Forge!" and headed into the wings as the British took the stage for the next scene. The director lifted Douglas right off of his feet and swung him in a circle. "You're *fantastic!*" he cried. "I *never* doubted you!" Then, setting his star down, he looked straight up and whispered to the heavens, "Thank you."

Looking grim, Douglas dusted off his uniform and hurried backstage.

Commando wiped his brow and realized he'd been sweating. He ducked into the costume room, where there was a sink. He splashed cold water on his face. It felt good.

As he dried off, he noticed a muffled sound of frenzied activity coming from the corner. He peered over his paper towel to see a pair of stockinged feet sticking out from behind a rack of clothing. Nearby sat a pair of boots — General Washington's boots.

"Doug?"

"I'm in a hurry," came the reply.

"Are you okay?" Intrigued, Commando stepped behind the rack. There stood Douglas, in his underwear from the waist down, plying a needle and thread, furiously sewing pockets into his uniform pants. He was stuffing the pockets with aces from a deck of cards that was fanned out on the floor.

Commando's jaw dropped. "You're going to do card tricks? Torrance'll have a heart attack!"

Douglas did not look up from his work. "I am determined to rescue this play."

"But it's going *great!*" Commando protested. "You're a big hit!"

"This will fit perfectly into the scene," the star promised, sewing madly, his nose on top of his work in the dim light. "I'll perform two quick card tricks in perfect silence, and when Mr. Torrance sees how much it improves the play, he'll be thrilled."

Commando listened to the voices from the stage. "Valley Forge is starting already. Will you make it?"

Douglas stood up. "Certainly I'll make it." He stepped into his trousers and attempted to pull them up to his waist. The left leg rose, but the right one was stuck. He yanked harder, but nothing moved. "Hmmmm."

Commando gawked. "You sewed your pants shut!"

It was all too true. Douglas' neat little stitches had attached the card pocket to the front *and* back of the pant leg. The opening was sealed tight.

His cue fast approaching, Doug flopped down on the floor in a concentrated effort to ram the leg through the obstruction. Try as he might, he could not kick his way into his pants.

Commando panicked. "Aw, Doug!" he gasped. "The play's going to be ruined, and it's all your fault!"

Douglas was highly insulted. "*My* fault?" he snorted, his postnasal drip returning rapidly. "Blame that paranoid drama teacher. If he hadn't been watching me like a hawk all evening, I could have taken my time and done a proper job!"

And then came the fateful words through the vent: "Attention! Here comes General Washington!"

Desperately, Commando joined the struggle, yanking on the uniform trousers while Douglas kicked like a horse.

"On three!" Douglas gasped. "One — two — three — !"

R-r-rip!

From the crotch to the back seam, the general's pants tore completely in half, leaving Commando holding one leg, and Douglas wearing the other.

"Get some pants!" cried Commando, but Douglas was already a step ahead of him, lunging at the clothes rack. Totally out of time, he snatched up the first pair of white trousers he set a hand on, pulling them right over the one pant leg he still wore.

"Not those!" Commando exclaimed, too late.

They were incredibly baggy, white with giant pink polka dots. Below the ankle, Douglas felt his feet slipping into enormous heavy plastic shoes. General Washington had selected clown pants, complete with big flat feet.

"Hang on, Doug! We'll find something!" Commando shouted, throwing himself at the costume rack, desperately searching for some pants — white, black, blue — anything but clown!

"Attention! Here comes General Washington!" repeated the actor onstage, this time a little nervously.

This was followed by Mr. Torrance's voice. "Fairchild, what are you doing? That's your cue!"

Out of options, Douglas ran for the stage, clown pants and all. The giant plastic shoes were so awkward that the first long stride threw him completely off balance, and he tumbled forward to the floor with an enormous crash. Dazed, he scrambled to his feet and made for Valley Forge, clomping loudly.

A confused murmur rippled through the audience.
Was General Washington on horseback? What else
made a *clop-clop-clop* sound, steadily growing in
volume? The Fairchilds looked at each other expectantly. Wouldn't that be spectacular?

Mr. Torrance caught up with Douglas in the wings.
The teacher opened his mouth, but his first sight of
the general struck him mute. Instead of speaking,
he sucked in air to the full capacity of both lungs. It
was a wheeze loud enough to be heard in the last
row of seats. He watched in helpless horror as
George Washington stepped out among his cold,
hungry troops at Valley Forge.

There was a shocked gasp from over four hundred
throats, followed by an instant of total silence, during
which Douglas' juicy throat clearing was magnified
by the sound system. All at once, a deafening roar
of laughter exploded in the auditorium. On the stage,
the other actors stared at their star in open-mouthed
amazement.

Commando raced to the wings, brandishing a
pair of navy-blue dress pants. "Hey, Doug, how
about these — ?" He pulled up, realizing it was too
late.

Still woozy from his big spill, Douglas became
aware of a small lump in his right shoe. With his
big toe, he felt the strange shape, not realizing
that he was stepping on the control button that
touched off the seventy-two mini-firecrackers sewn
into the insulated clown pants — thirty-six in each
leg.

General Washington went off like the Fourth of
July. Seventy-two rapid-fire explosions echoed
through the auditorium. Blue smoke billowed from

holes in the polka dot fabric. The audience went into hysterics. Shrieks of uncontrolled hilarity rang out.

Douglas threw himself to the floor of the stage, gurgling, *"The British are coming!"*

It brought the house down.

12

Guess Who's Coming to Dinner

"I would like to negotiate a discount on the grounds that this hamburger is defective."

The cashier sneered into Douglas' earnest face. "Hey, everybody, it's Bozo Washington, the famous actor and human bomb!"

"Twenty percent will be fine," said Douglas, unfazed.

"Yeah? Well, I want my discount from Friday. You left out all the good clown tricks. You didn't juggle bowling pins, or ride a unicycle, or give buzzer handshakes! You didn't even have a squirt flower!"

Sighing, Douglas paid up and went to a solitary spot at one of the long tables. He found no peace. Passing students identified him with nudges and winks, and moved off, laughing.

"That's him."

"That's George Washington."

"He's on the Twinkie Squad, you know."

"Man, I thought he'd be in the hospital! His pants exploded!"

"They let a *Twinkie* be George Washington?"

"Look at him!" seethed Beverly Busby from a nearby table. "He's acting like it's a normal day! He made fools of the whole school, *and* the father of our country, and he just sits there, writing in that stupid binder!"

Beverly was especially bitter. As Martha Washington, near the end of the play she had accompanied her husband to his tailor to order his inauguration suit. Her line had been:

"Make the trousers of good sturdy material. George is very hard on his clothes."

It was meant to add a human touch to the play. But for an audience that had just seen the general blow his pants off, it was the gag line of the evening. They had laughed poor Beverly off the stage. Now, three days later, she was still furious. "He's the Grand Twinkie of all Twinkies!"

Carol Stefanovich laughed. "Lighten up, Bev. When was the last time the school play got a standing ovation?"

"They're such losers!" Beverly raged on. "And yet *we*, the *cool* people, are always the ones who end up suffering! Well, I can't take it anymore! I know people who would have no problem taking these Twinkies and putting them in their place!"

"Who?"

"The Grand Knights of the Exalted Karpoozi!"

Carol laughed in her face. "These guys may — or may *not* — have set off a stink bomb three weeks ago, and to you, they're Robin Hood and his Merry Men!"

"That's not true," Beverly retorted smugly. "There were at least two stink bombs, plus the Willy and Milly thing, and clogging Silverman's toilet."

"Maybe," Carol conceded. "But it's getting to the point where every time the slightest thing goes wrong, people start saying it's a practical joke by the Grand Knights. On the way to the cafeteria, I saw this kid whose locker got kicked in. Everybody told him the Grand Knights did it. Or that school bus with the broken muffler — "

"That might have been them," Beverly argued.

"You don't even know if there *is* a 'them'!" Carol countered.

"Yes, I do, and what's more, they're going to help me get back at the Twinkies."

"You *definitely* don't know who they are," Carol pointed out.

Beverly smiled confidently. "Watch me."

The exterminator took one sniff in the principal's office and shook his head. "This ain't my job, man."

"But you said you handle rats and mice and small animals!" Mr. Silverman protested.

"We handle *live* rats and mice," replied the man. "We're exterminators. Whatever you got here is already exterminated." He started to walk away.

The principal moved after him, wringing his hands. "Well, who *do* we call?"

The exterminator shrugged. "You want to know my advice? Don't call nobody. Not unless you want to start knocking down walls to look for one little mess. Wait it out. In six weeks, whatever it is'll rot away and be gone — no charge."

"*Six weeks?!*" moaned Mr. Silverman. "We have children in this building! We can't wait six weeks!"

"Look," said the man, "there's one more chance. There's a small government office — the District of Columbia Ratcatcher. Give him a call. If he can't help you, nobody can."

"I appreciate your folks letting me stay over tonight," said Commando, riding home on the bus with Douglas that afternoon.

"Well, we have to give your dad time to study for the CPA exam tomorrow," Douglas replied. "This way he'll have the house all to himself so he can totally concentrate."

"I think he's going to pull an all-nighter," Commando said. He leaned back in his seat and exhaled heavily. "It's really weird to see your father sweating out school stuff."

"He'll do fine," said Douglas positively. "No one deserves it more than your dad. He's a great guy."

They got off the bus at Douglas' stop and entered the luxury apartment building, heading straight for the private elevator to the penthouse.

"Actually," said Commando as they began to ascend, "I'm afraid to leave him alone in the house all night. Who knows what boody traps I'll be walking into tomorrow? He could have the whole street wired to go off in my face."

Douglas shook his head in admiration. "The way you and your father do that is the most Pefkakian thing I've seen in the United States."

Commando raised an eyebrow. "What's so Pefkakian about father and son water bombings?"

"It's not the actual deed," Douglas explained. "It's the frolicking." The elevator door opened. "My family doesn't frolic nearly enough."

Commando laughed as they stepped out. "You could always try dropping a water balloon on your dad, just to see how he likes it." He grew alarmed at the look of delight on Douglas' face. "It was a *joke!*"

"Well, it shouldn't have been!" exclaimed Douglas. "I don't know why I didn't think of it long ago!"

"Because it's stupid!" Commando raved. "You don't booby-trap the greatest diplomat of the twentieth century!"

Douglas was offended. "Are you saying my father has no sense of humor?"

"No! But he's great, and dignified, and important! He dines with prime ministers, travels with royalty, and decides the fate of nations!"

But Douglas' mind was made up. "To you he's Ambassador Fairchild, but to me he's just — Dad. Plus he's in a great mood because the Helsinki trip went so well. This is the perfect time."

The Secret Service agent rode the private elevator up to the penthouse, his mirrored sunglasses hiding his alert eyes as they took in his surroundings. Of course, he knew that Ambassador Fairchild's home was perfectly safe. The President had dined here many times. But it was routine to check every room before the Chief Executive got there.

The elevator door opened, and he stepped off into the outer hall of the Fairchild residence. All seemed secure, except that the door to the apartment was slightly ajar. That was unusual. He pulled out a small walkie-talkie and put it to his lips.

"Door's open up here. Checking it out."

Cautiously, he pushed the door open. The plastic bucket Douglas and Commando had balanced there tipped over, depositing its cargo of lime Jell-O directly onto the Secret Service agent's head.

"Aaaaaah!"

Following years of training, he rolled across the floor, and came up, gun in hand. When he wiped the cold green slop from his sunglasses, he found himself holding at bay Douglas and Commando, both looking scared to death.

The walkie-talkie crackled to life. "What happened, Charlie? What's going on up there?"

The agent scrubbed at his face in outrage. "You're not going to *believe* this! A couple of kids just dumped a pail of Jell-O on me!"

Douglas snapped his fingers. "I forgot — it's Wednesday. The President's coming to dinner."

"Well, the President thought it was a pretty good joke," said Mrs. Fairchild as she and her husband prepared for bed that night.

"Why not?" replied the ambassador. "Nobody dropped Jell-O on him." He kicked off his slippers. "Be grateful for the Secret Service! Our Douglas could have slimed the leader of the Western world."

"I must have a word with him," said Mrs. Fairchild. "It was very thoughtless of him to invite a friend over, tonight of all nights."

"And did you hear the logic?" her husband raved. *"I* had a guest, so *he* was entitled to have one, too!

Mine was the President; his was *Commando*!"

"Actually, the President seemed quite impressed with Commando," Mrs. Fairchild observed. "The boy has a real grasp of foreign policy."

"He has great ideas," the ambassador admitted. "So do I. I wish I'd had the chance to express some of them at my own dinner table. He *hogged* the President! Heaven knows what the press would do if they found out that our Scandinavian policy is being set by an eleven-year-old with spiked hair and a snake earring!"

She laughed. "What if the press found out that Ambassador Fairchild's all-American son is really a Pefkakian foreign national?"

Her husband grinned in spite of himself. "Hah! He's about as Pefkakian as the President! If it weren't for that stupid birth certificate, he would never even have found out!" He switched off the light, but turned it on again a second later. He sat bolt-upright, looking startled. "We're losing sight of the most important thing! That Jell-O was meant for *me*!"

13

Karpoozi Is Not in the Dictionary

Commando walked on air all the next day. "Dad, you're not going to believe it!" he raved into the pay phone. "I met the President! . . . of the United States! . . . Yeah! I sat right next to him! And he liked me — !"

"Give me that!" Douglas wrenched the receiver from Commando's hand. "Mr. Rivera? This is Douglas Fairchild speaking. How did your exam go? Did you use my example of the Pefkakian economy in the essay question?"

Commando grabbed the phone back. "Dad? So we were talking about Scandinavian trade, right? He loved my ideas!"

"Do you think you passed?" bellowed Douglas right in Commando's ear.

Commando listened for a minute. "That hard, huh? Well, you knew your stuff. Take it easy, Dad. I'll be home right after — uh — practice."

" 'Bye, Mr. Rivera!" hollered Douglas.

Commando hung up, and the two headed for the conference room.

"Poor Dad," said Commando. "He won't get the results for a whole week. He'll be freaking by then."

The Special Discussion group was already assembled when the two arrived. Martin Richardson was waiting for Douglas with murder in his eye. "Douglas, what is the meaning of this?" In his hand he held the taped-together Grand Knights sign-up sheet.

Douglas was horrified. "What is it doing here? It's supposed to be on the bulletin board!"

"It's *supposed* to be in the garbage!" Martin seethed.

"But I thought I made it clear," Douglas persisted. "Without open membership, we can't be the Grand Knights of the Exalted Karpoozi."

Martin pulled at his hair. "I can't believe you're starting this again! You're not Grand Knights because there *are* no Grand Knights!"

"I'm a Grand Knight," came Gerald Dooley's timid little voice. He reached into his shirt and pulled out his membership card.

"Yeah, me, too," put in Dave. "Except that Willy ate my card. Or was it Milly . . . ?"

"We can get you a replacement," offered Douglas.

"Can mine be in lavender?" asked Anita.

Martin seemed too stunned to speak, so Julia took over. "Well, let's just say that we *are* — uh — a little club. We still wouldn't be able to accept new members, because we're also a counseling group."

"But I've already explained that it's impossible for anyone to sign up," said Douglas patiently. "It's been on the bulletin board for weeks, and we haven't had a single name."

"Is that right!" snarled Martin. The guidance counsellor held out the sign-up sheet. In the space by the Roman numeral I was a signature — *Beverly Busby*. "Okay, smart guy, what do you say to *this*?"

Douglas regarded the paper. "Hmmm."

Commando read over his shoulder. "Beverly Busby!? She hates our guts!" He grinned. "If she finds out it's us, she'll drop dead!"

"How can you say there's no Grand Knights?" Ric demanded of Martin. "Would Beverly Busby sign up for nothing?"

"We must be pretty happening if *she* wants to join," agreed Dave.

Martin held up his hands for order. "Calm down, everybody. Nobody's joining anything. We're going to tell Beverly we're the Special Discussion Group, not some club."

"I don't see what all the fuss is about," said Douglas. "This is really very simple. Leave it to me."

"To *you*?" Martin exploded. "It's your fault we're in this mess!"

"We'll have to put this to a vote," Douglas decided. "And if memory serves, Mr. and Mrs. Richardson are nonvoting associate members."

A secret ballot was held, and when the dust cleared, Douglas had been elected president, chairman of the board, and membership coordinator.

Martin swallowed hard. "We think it's great that you kids want to take charge of your own affairs. Douglas, can you handle it?"

"Certainly," said the president of the Grand Knights.

*   *   *

When Commando arrived at school the next day, he found a commotion going on outside the guidance office. People were crowded around the bulletin board, shouting, pointing, and laughing. The mood was somewhere between hilarity and astonishment.

Commando pushed his way through the crowd. The focus of attention was the sign-up sheet for the Grand Knights of the Exalted Karpoozi. It had been put back in the display, but on top of Beverly Busby's signature, someone had written in three-inch letters of fluorescent pink Magic Marker:

* * REJECTED * *

The crowd parted to admit Beverly herself, student council president and homecoming queen, dropping by to check on the status of her sign-up. The fatal word jumped off the sheet at her like a ravening tiger.

"Aaaaaah!" yelped Beverly, jumping back in horrified shock.

Commando laughed out loud with the pure joy of it. Good old Doug had struck again. He'd promised to take care of it, and here it was, taken care of in style. There was only one thing funnier than Beverly Busby signing up for the Twinkie Squad — and that was Beverly Busby signing up for the Twinkie Squad and being told no dice.

Beverly turned blazing eyes on Commando. "What's so funny, Twinkie?"

"They must be pretty exclusive, Bev," he said with a shrug. "Either that, or you're slipping."

Kahlil put an arm around Beverly's shoulders. "Yo, who cares?" He dismissed the sheet on the bulletin board with a wave of his hand. "Bunch of snobs!"

Beverly backed away from the bulletin board, never taking her murderous gaze from the bright pink rejection.

Throughout the day, the guidance bulletin board was a constant attraction. Commando went out of his way to walk by at all class changes. Not only did nobody try to remove the sheet, but there was always a large crowd on hand — not laughing, or cheering, or even showing outrage on Beverly's behalf. They gathered in small groups like people do at funerals, speaking in hushed tones.

"I can't believe they rejected Beverly Busby! What do you have to do to get in?"

"They're a really happening club! They built the ultimate stink bomb!"

"They pulled off the Willy and Milly thing."

"They clogged Silverman's toilet!"

"They hang out with movie stars!"

"Think I could get in?"

"Are you kidding? They rejected *Beverly Busby!*"

"I wonder who they are — ?"

For the first time in over a month, Commando was actually looking forward to three-thirty. By the time he reached the conference room, Douglas was handing out replacement membership cards, including a lavender one for Anita.

"I've got some Grand Knights business," piped Commando. "I say we all give Douglas a standing ovation for the way he handled the Beverly Busby thing." The Grand Knights of the Exalted Karpoozi leaped to their feet, clapping and cheering.

That was how the Richardsons found them moments later. Martin and Julia had a different opinion of Douglas Fairchild. Julia looked a little pale, but Martin was red-hot steaming mad.

"Are you crazy, Douglas?" he roared, the sign-up sheet clutched in his fist. "You said you were going to handle this!"

"It's handled," said Douglas mildly. "All the *voting* members approved."

"You can't write *REJECTED* in giant pink letters and hang it on a wall for everybody to see! You humiliated the poor girl!"

Douglas shrugged. "She could either be accepted or rejected. You said we couldn't take anybody new, so we rejected her."

"There were nicer ways to do it, Douglas," put in Julia. "You have a little talk with the girl — "

"What we're squabbling over is the method," Douglas interrupted. "The end result is the same. She's off our case, and no one is trying to get into the Grand Knights."

Martin slammed the sheet down on the conference table. "Oh, yeah? Well, how about this?" On the crumpled paper, under Beverly Busby's rejected signature, were dozens of new names, right up to number XXXVII.

The Grand Knights all gathered around. Commando pointed to line II, right under Beverly's name. "That's Kahlil! This morning he called us snobs; now he's the first guy to try and get himself in!"

"Hmmm," was Douglas' only comment.

"That's easy for you to say!" snarled Martin. "What do we do now?"

"Well, obviously, we have to reject the whole lot," Douglas reasoned.

Violently, Martin crumpled up the paper and slam-dunked it into the garbage. "And you'd better not iron that and put it back up!"

Gerald was devastated. "You mean we can't be Grand Knights anymore?"

"There's no such thing as Grand Knights!" roared Martin. "It's — it's — how do you describe it? It's a *non-thing!*"

"Actually," Douglas began, "in Pefkakia — "

"That's another subject I don't want to hear about!" The guidance counsellor turned on Douglas. "And if I so much as see you in the vicinity of that bulletin board, you're dead! Got it?"

The emergency meeting was called for seven A.M. in the vacant lot behind the school.

Gerald looked around. "Where's Douglas?"

Commando rubbed his eyes and yawned hugely. "For his sake, I hope he gets here soon. If I got up in the middle of the night for nothing — !"

"I know!" growled Yolanda. "I rented six movies last night, and I could only see four 'cause I had to get up so early!"

"I'm here by now, anyway," said Dave. "Mr. Poppolini put me in charge of feeding Willy and Milly."

At that moment, the window of a rear classroom was raised and out swung a long leg. Douglas eased himself over the sill, and set about climbing the chain-link fence that surrounded the school property. Under his arm he carried a thick sheaf of paper.

The group raced to meet him. "You're late," growled Commando.

Douglas jumped to the ground. "I calculated it to the second, but I forgot that the photocopier takes three minutes to warm up." He separated his papers into seven equal stacks, and handed one to each person, keeping one for himself.

Commando stared. The sheet read:

The Grand Knights of the Exalted Karpoozi
regret to announce
that membership is closed forthwith.
We appreciate your interest
and hope that at a later date
we will be able to consider new applications.

"These go on every locker in the school," Douglas explained.

"But Mr. Richardson said there *is* no Grand Knights," protested Anita.

Douglas shrugged impatiently. "How could there be no Grand Knights? I'm a Grand Knight — you're a Grand Knight." He pointed at Thaddeus G. Little. "I can say the school doesn't exist. That doesn't make it disappear in a puff of smoke."

"We exist!" said Gerald, ecstatic. He had been up late last night, feeling sad that he'd finally managed to get a membership card only to be told he was a member of nothing.

"Grand Knights or not," said Commando skeptically, "my main man Martin is going to have a cow when he sees this! You promised to cut it out."

"On the contrary," said Douglas. "My promise was exactly this: that I would not be seen *by him* in the vicinity of the guidance bulletin board."

"It makes perfect sense to me," said Ric, hanging off the fence. "We have to explain to those people why they can't join."

"It's only fair," added Anita.

"You guys remember these arguments for when Martin hits the roof," Commando advised.

There were more than eight hundred students at Thaddeus G. Little Middle School, so it took the seven over an hour to distribute their papers. By the eight-forty bell, the lockers were plastered with notices, and the Grand Knights of the Exalted Karpoozi had snuck out and melted into the student body milling around in the playground.

The Grand Knights were big news. What two days ago had been wild rumors of stink bombs and practical jokers had blossomed into the school craze and the school mystery. Every leak in a bicycle tire was suspect. Could this be the work of the Grand Knights? Students gathered together in groups in the hallways to pool their information.

1. No one had heard of the Grand Knights until the sign-up sheet had appeared on the bulletin board.

2. Rumors linked the Grand Knights with the smell in the school and at least twenty-five other practical jokes, but nothing could be confirmed, because no one knew a Grand Knight.

3. No one knew what "Karpoozi" meant, and it wasn't in the dictionary.

4. The Grand Knights were very exclusive, since they'd rejected Bevery Busby.

5. Anybody who could somehow manage to get in would become an instant superstar at Thaddeus G. Little.

Speculation ran high. There were Grand Knights among the student body, faces that you saw every day! Your best friend could be a Grand Knight, and you might never know! Some thought there were as many as a hundred members; other estimates ranged as low as three. One popular theory was that it was a secret club from the high school, now re-cruiting eighth-graders for next year. A few students were even suggesting that Beverly Busby *was* a Grand Knight, and had arranged her own rejection to throw people off the scent.

"Are you kidding?" was Beverly's reaction. "I wouldn't give the skin off a grape to those snobs! Besides, they're not allowed to keep people out! This is a public school!"

Carol raised an eyebrow. "You try to shut the Twin-kie Squad out of things every time you get a chance."

"That's different," said Beverly smugly. "I mean, *we're* normal."

"Why don't you just admit it?" laughed Carol. "You want to be a Grand Knight so bad it's killing you!"

Beverly scowled at her. "Of course not! But if I did, I'd have no problem getting in."

"That's not what the bulletin board said."

"My mother is the president of the PTA," snapped Beverly, "and Mr. Silverman is scared to death of her! I'm going to get her to complain that there's an elitist club at the school! Then they'll have to let everybody in, or close up!"

Mr. Richardson stood in the doorway of the con-ference room, holding one of the flyers. "All right," he said, looking straight at Douglas. "Who wrote this?"

Douglas stood up. "I did."

"Well — " began Martin angrily.

"He's lying!" interrupted a voice. Martin's head snapped up. Commando was on his feet, looking defiant. "Doug didn't do it; I did."

"Now, Armando — " began Julia soothingly.

"It was me!" Gerald Dooley sprang up. "These guys didn't do anything!"

Martin was bewildered. "Now just a minute!"

"I wrote it!" cried Anita.

"And I helped!" added Ric.

"Don't believe them!" begged Dave. "It's all *my* fault!"

"Ya got me with the goods!" Yolanda confessed, back in gangster mode.

"Sit down, all of you!" Martin ordered tersely. And when they were all settled back in their chairs, he continued, "This meeting of the *Special Discussion Group* will come to order. Now, who'd like to begin this afternoon?"

The silence was ear-splitting. Even Julia seemed cowed.

"Gerald?" Martin prompted.

But Gerald drew his neck in like a turtle and shook his head.

"Yolanda? Seen any good movies lately?"

Yolanda leaned back in her chair and put her feet up on the conference table, but said nothing.

Martin played his trump card. "Douglas — tell us a little more about Pefkakia."

But even Douglas had nothing to say. Helplessly, Martin looked to his wife for chitchat.

"Uh — " she began, "the smell in the school seems to be getting worse. Do you think they'll ever find it?"

No reply, no comment.

"Well — I hear they're having some kind of specialist come in tomorrow," said Martin finally, just to fill in the silence.

That was how it went. The Richardsons had a conversation until four-fifteen. The Grand Knights of the Exalted Karpoozi weren't talking.

14

Ratcatcher

The District of Columbia Ratcatcher arrived to find the Thaddeus G. Little office a beehive of activity. Although the principal's door was kept shut with a towel jammed into the crack, the smell had definitely spread. Air fresheners were everywhere, on desks and stuck to walls. The school secretary had convinced her brother, a Pennsylvania miner, to send her a charcoal dust filter, which she wore over her nose and mouth all day, even when on the telephone. Other office workers tried scented handkerchiefs, and even swimmers' nose plugs.

Mr. Silverman had a damp dish towel pressed against his face, which gave him the look of a doctor about to perform surgery. His voice was muffled and nasal as he spoke on the phone. "No, Mrs. Busby, I don't have a cold. We have some smell problems here . . . now, what's so important? . . . The Grand Knights of the Exalted *what*?"

"Ratcatcher," announced the man from the city.

"Just a moment, please," said Mr. Silverman. Into the phone he went on, "Mrs. Busby, I never heard of any club like that."

The secretary with the charcoal mask called across to him. "Mr. Silverman, I have one of the parents on the line. Do we have a club called the Knights of Jacuzzi?"

"Ratcatcher," repeated the man, louder this time.

"Would you just *wait* a minute!" exclaimed the principal. "Mrs. Busby, I assure you that all school clubs are open to anyone who wants to join."

"Listen, pal," said the Ratcatcher impatiently, "I got field mice in the Smithsonian, fruit bats in Georgetown, and someone on the Mall saw something that sounds like it might be a baby stegasaurus. Did you call for the Ratcatcher, or what?"

"Oh, the *Ratcatcher!*" cried Mr. Silverman, dropping the phone with a clatter. "Thank goodness you're here! We have this terrible smell!"

"I got a nose," the man acknowledged.

From the telephone, Beverly Busby's mother could be heard shouting. This was followed by a sharp click.

"Come into my office," said Mr. Silverman. "That's where it seems to be the worst."

"No!" chorused the office workers as he moved to open the door.

"Mr. Silverman," piped the secretary, "you've got another call about those Grand Knights. This father says his son's very upset that he can't join."

The Ratcatcher marched into the inner office, sniffing experimentally. "I don't know what you got here," he announced loudly. "Smells like a whale swam up your pipes and died!"

Mr. Silverman was mystified. "Have you ever heard of any Grand Knights?" he asked his staff.

"There were notices about them yesterday," put in a file clerk.

"Mrs. Busby's back on line four. She sounds mad."

"Oh, boy. I'll take it." He started for the phone.

"Hey, you — principal," called the Ratcatcher. "We gotta work out a strategy."

Mr. Silverman held his head. "What strategy? Find the dead rat, and get it out of here!"

"You got places maybe we shouldn't go? Classes we shouldn't disturb?"

"There's another call on line three — those Grand Knights again."

Mr. Silverman moaned into his dish towel. "Do whatever you have to do! I want my school back!"

The Ratcatcher's men fell upon Thaddeus G. Little Middle School like a swarm of bees. They blanketed the building, tapping, and sniffing, and studying the engineering maps. Still, Douglas' Pefkakian lunch, built into the ceiling of the home ec room, managed to elude them.

They returned after lunch with the heavy artillery — portable X ray machines. Whole classes were evacuated by men in lead suits. Large radiation screens were set up.

"This is stupid!" exclaimed Mr. Silverman as he and his office staff were marched out into the hall. "It's a *smell*! How can you X-ray for it?"

"If you got a dead animal," explained the Rat-catcher patiently, "its bones show up on the X ray. Then you know where it is, and you go get it."

"Mr. Silverman," called the secretary, "it's Mrs. Shura from the school board. They've been getting complaints about the Grand Knights."

"I'll — I'll call her back," said the harassed principal. He turned to the Ratcatcher. "We've got kind of a crisis here. There's this club, the Grand Knights — forget it. There's no explaining it. Couldn't you maybe work around us here?"

The Ratcatcher gazed at him pityingly. "Look, Einstein, here is where it stinks. You want us to X-ray the half of the building that's okay?"

But since the Ratcatcher's men were looking for a skeleton, and the squid is a boneless creature, the X rays of the ceiling of the home ec room and the floor of Mr. Silverman's office turned up nothing.

"You mean that's *it?*" screamed poor Mr. Silverman as the Ratcatcher and his men packed up to leave. "Isn't there something else you can do? Some other kind of equipment you can use?"

"Sure," said the Ratcatcher. "It's called a sledgehammer."

"What?"

"Face it — the next step is to break walls." He took pity on the principal's agony. "Don't get excited. Not the whole building. We've narrowed it down to a few rooms." He grinned. "Your office is one of them. We bash in the walls, and when we find your problem, we get rid of it."

"And if you don't find it?"

The Ratcatcher shrugged. "Then you get new walls. Look, you got no choice. Free up the rooms, and give us a call when you're ready."

The caravan of trucks marked *D.C. Dept. of Health* pulled out of the parking lot and headed down G Street to the city garage. They drove right past Douglas and Commando, who were on their way to the Rivera house after school. Special Discussion Group had been cancelled because Mr. Silverman had called an emergency staff meeting.

"Oh, man, Doug!" Commando groaned, pointing at the trucks. "The whole city's looking for your dumb squid!"

"They're unbelievably incompetent," said Douglas critically. "A child could have found it by now."

"I hope *no one* finds it!" said Commando feelingly. "Because if they do, and they somehow pin it on us, we're toast!"

The forty-nine teachers, administrators, counsellors, clerks, and janitors of Thaddeus G. Little Middle School were packed into the music room.

"Is this about those idiots who were poking around all day?" demanded Nurse Chung. "I had a kid with a hundred-and-three fever in my office — they started banging on the pipes with wrenches!"

"I was showing a film in the lab," Mr. Poppolini complained. "Those guys barged in and plunked a lead wall down right in front of the projector! They said they were X-raying the room next door."

All at once, a babble of protest rose up.

"All right, all right." Mr. Silverman put his hands up for order. "This has nothing to do with dead rats and lead walls. I spent the whole day on the phone with enraged parents. There's a revolution brewing over some club that's elitist and snobbish and putting everybody down. At least, that's what the parents are telling me. My problem is I never heard of this so-called club! Does *anybody* know *anything* about the Grand Knights of the Exalted Karpoozi?"

There was dead silence, punctuated by twin gasps from the Richardsons.

"Oh, no!" groaned Martin. "It's *us*!"

Mr. Silverman was appalled. "You and Julia?"

"No! Our kids! The Special Discussion Group!"

"The Twinkie Squad?" chorused everybody.

"Your kids know about the Grand Knights?" the principal asked eagerly.

"Our kids *are* the Grand Knights! One of them started pretending that we're some kind of social club, and it just caught on."

"Yeah, but the 'Exalted Karpoozi'?"

"It's Pefkakian," Julia supplied.

"Fairchild!" chorused half a dozen people in the room. Anyone who came into contact with Douglas usually heard a lot about Pefkakia.

"Well, he's opened up a real can of worms here," said Mr. Silverman sourly. "Now you're going to have to take everybody who wants in. And from what I hear, that means *everybody*!"

"We can't do that," said Martin. "We cancelled the Grand Knights as of yesterday."

"Well, as of tomorrow, they're back in business. These parents expect to see their kids become members. You should have heard Mrs. Busby! She accused me of running a country club!"

Martin looked helpless. "Wouldn't it be easier just to explain that the whole thing is a hoax? We'll have to sign up hundreds of people for nothing!"

"I'd rather sign up *millions* of people than have

to explain about Pefkakia!" said the principal positively. "We'd all look like idiots!" He took a deep
breath. "I say we throw it open and have a mass
meeting of the Grand Knights. In a couple of weeks,
everybody'll figure out that the club does nothing,
and it'll die out on its own."

"Eight hundred new members?" exclaimed Ric.
"We gotta get more chairs!"

The Richardsons had just told the Special Discussion Group that they could be Grand Knights
again — indeed, that they had no choice.

"This is great!" breathed Anita. "*Us* in front of the
whole school!"

"It's not very Pefkakian," said Douglas disapprov-
ingly. "These new people know nothing about Ano
Pefki and our great traditions." Of course, neither
did Douglas, though pointing it out would only com-
plicate matters.

"Look," said Martin, "this one comes straight from
the top, so don't even think about arguing. We got
the school into this, and we're going to get the school
out."

The new sign-up sheet was the first order of business, and it went up immediately. It covered the
entire bulletin board. At the top, Douglas wrote:

*Grand Knights Membership Drive — Admittance
Guaranteed (No Rejections)*

It was jammed with signatures by noon the next
day.

Douglas wasn't satisfied. "We need more public-
ity," he decided.

"What for?" asked Martin. "The whole world joined
up."

"There are exactly five hundred and seventy-six signatures," Douglas countered. "Thaddeus G. Little has an enrollment of eight hundred and eleven. Excluding us, that leaves two hundred and twenty-eight students we still need to reach."

So Mr. Silverman made P.A. announcements, and the group began work on giant posters:

DON'T MISS YOUR ONE CHANCE
BECAUSE WE'RE REALLY CHOOSY.
WE'RE THE GRAND KNIGHTS OF
THE EXALTED KARPOOZI
GENERAL MEETING — FRIDAY, 3:30

New sign-up sheets were taped to the wall beside the bulletin board. Almost immediately, they were covered with names. The Grand Knights now had seven hundred and ninety-two new members. Out of eight hundred and eleven students, all but twelve had enrolled in the club that had started out as the school joke — the Special Discussion Group.

The question became: Would all those people fit in the Thaddeus G. Little gym?

"Well, surely they won't all come," said Mr. Silverman. "Will they?"

"I've been asking around," said Martin Richardson nervously. "I've yet to find a single kid who isn't planning on being there."

"Sure, they say that *now*. But life goes on. They have their friends, their families. And don't forget — midterms go home today. By Friday, half of them will have forgotten they're Grand Knights."

But not even midterm report cards could divert the minds of seven hundred and ninety-two Grand

Knights of the Exalted Karpoozi. Schedules were rearranged, dental appointments cancelled. Conversation centered almost completely on Friday's meeting. What would happen there? Who would the original Grand Knights turn out to be? How did Beverly Busby fit in? How long would the smell be allowed to go on? What would the next big practical joke be? Students pondered everything, right down to the correct wardrobe for the big event.

"All I know," said Commando, shooting baskets in the schoolyard, "is that eight hundred kids are going to walk into the gym, see *us* on the stage, and realize they signed up for the Twinkie Squad. We're going to have a major freak-out on our hands!"

Douglas was keeping him company until the bus came. "I can't figure out those twelve people who didn't sign up," he said in perplexity. "How can they pass up a chance to be Grand Knights?"

Commando popped an eight-footer. "Maybe they've been sick the last few days. Of course, maybe they've just got some brains."

"What are your plans for this evening?" Douglas inquired. "I'm feeling some good booby-trap ideas coming on."

Commando missed an easy shot. "Not tonight, man. I don't think tonight's going to be a fun time at my house."

"Why?"

"My midterm," Commando sighed. "It says I'm off the team for beating up on a guy."

"But I'm the guy," Douglas reminded him. "I'll explain it to your dad."

"Yeah, but then there's the problem of me lying to him all these weeks."

Douglas looked thoughtful. "You could always lose your midterm. You know — a brisk wind can blow it clear into Virginia. It happens every day."

Commando shook his head. "You have to get it signed and bring it back." He looked depressed. "Besides, my dad's exam is over. It's only a matter of time before he wants to come to a basketball game. Then I'll have to tell him for sure."

Douglas took out his own midterm.

"Four C's, three D's, and an F," he clucked. "Lucky for me I'm Pefkakian."

"But your American half is going to get its butt kicked," said Commando. He sighed. "I'll stall. At least until after my dad finds out whether he's a CPA or not." He took a deep breath. "I sure hope he passed!"

Douglas unlocked his desk drawer and reverently pulled out the Surgeon General's letter. He allowed his eyes to caress the most important signature in American medicine.

Commando had made him promise not to use this irrefutable evidence, but now Douglas had no choice. It was the only way to prove that his friend had not attacked him at recess that day.

Into his typewriter he fitted a business envelope, which he addressed to Mr. Silverman. Commando would be furious, but he'd thank him for this in the end. This evidence would reach Mr. Silverman before Commando planned to come clean to his father. Well then, by confession time, Commando would be cleared, and there would be nothing to confess.

He sealed the letter and took it to his father's study.

There he slipped it into the middle of the pile of mail to be delivered the next day by special courier.

"What are you doing?"

Douglas wheeled. His father stood in the hallway, blocking his escape. "I was just looking around. I live here, too, you know."

The ambassador examined the top of the doorway and the ceiling over it. "Is there a bucket of Jell-O anywhere waiting for me?" Gingerly, he darted into his study in a crablike crouch. "Safe!"

"Don't be sarcastic," said Douglas. "I still think you need to frolic more."

Mr. Fairchild sat down at his desk. "Ambassadors don't frolic."

"Mr. Rivera frolics," said Douglas.

The ambassador held his head. "Mr. Rivera sets booby traps, and Mr. Rivera likes hamburgers, and and Mr. Rivera is 'one of the guys.' He also must be twenty years younger than I am. What can I tell you, Douglas? I'm not Mr. Rivera."

"I didn't mean it that way," said Douglas kindly. "What you do is fine, too. Good night." And he went off, leaving his father clawing at the desk blotter.

15

Hereby, Forthwith, and All That Other Stuff

"Hello, I need a ratcatcher . . . very funny . . . all right, I'll hold."

It was Friday morning, and Mr. Silverman was back in his broom closet.

As Muzak was piped through the receiver, the secretary burst in, her charcoal filter mask flipped up on the top of her head. She tossed an envelope onto the desk. "This came by courier," she said coldly, and stormed out. The office staff was growing less patient every day. They felt that the principal should suffer with the troops instead of escaping to this cramped, but breathable, closet.

Mr. Silverman picked up the envelope and stared. The return address read: *The Surgeon General of the United States of America.* Was the smell in the school such a health hazard that word had reached the Surgeon General's office? He was about to open the letter when the Muzak stopped, and a voice on the line said "Yeah?"

"Yes! Are you a ratcatcher? . . . Oh, hello again. I'm glad it's you. Listen, I can't stand it anymore. The students can't concentrate, my staff's in revolt, and the janitor's threatened to resign. I left a jacket on my coat rack, and now the smell won't come out. I've had it dry-cleaned *four times!* Knock in walls, ceilings! Knock in the whole school, for all I care! But *get rid of that smell!*" By this time, he was standing up, howling into the phone. "I'm sorry for yelling . . . yes, I realize ratcatchers have feelings, too . . . this weekend? Excellent! Thank you! Really, I can't thank you enough! Thank — yes, fine. 'Bye."

He hung up and ripped open the envelope. His jaw dropped. He gawked at the Surgeon General's letter. It was unbelievable! That signature was *real* — either that, or an almost perfect copy. It was impossible that Armando Rivera had access to either the Surgeon General or an expert forger!

Douglas Fairchild! His father's connections would extend to the Surgeon General and far beyond. But why would Douglas go to such great lengths to clear Armando? Mr. Silverman thought back to Douglas' attempt to blame the whole thing on a basketball. Was he being threatened by Armando? Still?

The principal's head was spinning. If this letter *was* from Douglas, how had he convinced his father — let alone the *Surgeon General* — to go along with such an obvious ruse?

Mr. Silverman struggled to make sense of it. For a brief moment, he even considered the possibility that the Surgeon General, on a fluke, had heard of Armando's case, examined the victim, and had this to say. Now, that was *really* crazy! The smell in the school was affecting his brain!

One thing was certain. This was far too serious to be discussed with Armando and Douglas. He picked up the phone and called his secretary half a school away. "I need to see Mrs. Fairchild and Mr. Rivera. As soon as possible — today, if they can make it. Tell them it's urgent."

"Martin, I haven't been this nervous since our wedding day."

It was three-twenty-five, and the Richardsons were on their way to the gym, where the giant meeting of the Grand Knights was to be held.

Martin sighed. "We've lost control, that's for sure." He looked at his wife earnestly. "It isn't our fault, Julia. It's just Douglas. No one can handle him. His father shapes world destiny every day, but can't keep a leash on his own lousy kid!"

"I don't mean *that!*" His wife looked sad. "Armando was right. To the rest of the school, our kids are nothing more than the Twinkie Squad — "

"Hey — " Martin interrupted.

"I'm not saying I like it! I'm just saying it's *true!* What if eight hundred children see our group up there and laugh them off the stage? It would crush a boy like Gerald — just when he's starting to come out of his shell. All the progress of the last two months — "

"What progress?" Martin exploded. "They're members of a non-club that does nothing!"

"But it's *their* non-club, and it's given them a sense of belonging, and togetherness, and responsibility. It's given them a feeling for who they are. And now that's all going to be blown to pieces because, in the end, to this school they're Twinkies — nothing more, nothing less."

Martin stopped and took her hand. "Maybe it won't happen that way."

His wife regarded him intently. "Do you *really* believe that?"

The bell rang, but it interrupted no answer from Martin Richardson.

The usual three-thirty traffic in the halls was replaced by a stampede for the gym. If any student had somehow forgotten the meeting, the pandemonium in the corridors served as a sure reminder. By three-thirty-five, the gym was jam-packed, the atmosphere supercharged. Excited voices echoed all around. Students attempted to sneak closer to the stage. Fist fights broke out, but these were soon stopped. No one wanted to risk spending the meeting in the principal's office and missing out on the Grand Knights.

Backstage, the Richardsons were preparing the Special Discussion Group for their big moment in the spotlight. The only jitters seemed to belong to the guidance counsellors. Julia in particular was almost in tears as she straightened Gerald's tie.

"You look very handsome," she smiled bravely. Gerald wore his best suit, now badly rumpled from a day spent wadded up in his locker.

Dave wore a proper collared shirt, rather than his usual ripped-up T-shirt. Ric was actually subdued. Apparently, it was possible for him to become too nervous to fidget. The girls both wore tons of makeup. Anita's cheeks would have glowed in the dark, and the smeared mascara around Yolanda's eyes made her look like a raccoon.

"Listen, everyone," Julia announced. "You all look wonderful. We're very proud of you. Right, Martin?"

Martin, who wasn't proud of anything or anybody and wanted to get this whole idiotic episode over with, nodded reluctantly.

"No matter what happens out there," Julia continued, "please remember that you're very special people. No one can take that from you."

Commando frowned. Why was Julia so open-handed with compliments today? She wasn't *happy*. She seemed more *terrified* than anything else. All at once, he had the answer. "You think they're going to laugh us off the stage, don't you?"

Julia turned to him, her eyes open and earnest. For the first time, it hit Commando that the Richardsons really *did* care. Sure, they were out of touch — maybe even not too bright. Sure, they were accomplishing absolutely nothing in their forty-five minutes a day, except grinning and garbage. But at least these two goofy guidance counsellors *liked* their Twinkies, and didn't want to see them hurt. How about that! The Richardsons weren't such bad guys after all!

Martin regarded Douglas. "I know you're not going to tell me what you're planning to say to all these people. Just please — *please* — don't do anything crazy!"

"You have my word as a Pefkakian," replied the president of the Grand Knights.

Mr. Silverman entered the backstage area. He looked daggers at Douglas and Commando.

"Douglas, Armando," he greeted them icily. The Surgeon General's letter was still fresh in his mind.

Commando was mystified. Now what?

The principal went onstage first, grabbing the microphone in a squeal of feedback. "Before I introduce the — uh" — his face twisted — "*officers* of your new club, I want to mention that today's meeting is co-sponsored by the PTA."

The audience was rowdy, the noise level growing.

"Now I'd like to turn things over to the people you're really here to see." There was an enormous cheer. The principal swallowed hard. "Please welcome your fellow Grand Knights of the — "

The audience went berserk. Eight hundred students simultaneously leaped to their feet, and an earsplitting cheer went up in the gym.

" — Exalted Karpoozi," muttered Mr. Silverman. He replaced the mike in its stand and slunk off to the wings amid the thunderous ovation.

The frenzied shrieks, screams, foot stomping, and applause soon resolved itself into a resounding chant: *"Grand Knights!... Grand Knights!... Grand Knights!"*

With great dignity, Douglas led the Special Discussion Group onto the stage. Instantly, silence fell, as though someone had pulled the plug on eight hundred throats. Over the quiet, rang the half-demented voice of Beverly Busby from the front row. *"The Twinkie Squad!"*

Carol laughed right in Beverly's face. "How about that, Bev? *You* signed up to be a Twinkie!"

"No-o-o-o!" Beverly wailed.

The students watched in bewilderment as Douglas led his group to the microphone. How could the

Grand Knights, the most exclusive, glamorous, trendy club there was — turn out to be the school losers, the geeks, the weirdos? How could eight hundred students be so *wrong*? Murmurs rippled through the shocked crowd.

"That guy's a Twinkie!"

"Twinkie, my foot! That's the whole squad!"

"It's George Washington!"

"It's the guy from the sports building wall!"

"Yeah, but the *Twinkie Squad*?"

Douglas leaned over to the microphone. "Greetings. On behalf of the Grand Knights of the Exalted Karpoozi, welcome to our new members."

No response. The surprise was beginning to wear off. Commando surveyed faces in the crowd. Blank expressions solidified into sneers, puzzled frowns into belligerent glares. Julia had been right. The students were going to cut them to pieces. It gave Commando a sick sensation in the pit of his stomach. He didn't feel badly for himself, and Doug sure wouldn't care. He was sorry for Gerald, Dave, Yolanda, Ric, and Anita. Out of the corner of his eye, he could see Gerald beside him, glowing with pride as Douglas spoke about the club and its Pefkakian name. The Grand Knights *was* nothing. But somewhere between dumping perfume in air vents, chasing after gerbils, and drilling holes in Silverman's floor, the nothing had turned into *something*! Together they had faced problems, fought off disasters, climbed mountains. And now they were about to be crushed — by the entire school, no less. Even Doug couldn't talk the Grand Knights out of this one!

". . . and now that you understand our great traditions," Douglas was saying, "you'll also understand what I must do. This organization cannot have eight hundred members and still be true to the spirit of the immortal Ano Pefki. Therefore, I hereby resign the presidency, and relinquish my membership in the Grand Knights, forthwith."

A shocked murmur buzzed through the crowd. Resign? Now? But things were just getting started!

The Richardsons leaned forward in the wings, spellbound.

"Douglas, what do you think you're doing?" hissed Mr. Silverman.

The other members of the Special Discussion Group stared at Douglas in shock — all except Commando. He knew that Douglas had just hit on the one way out of this. An enormous grin split his face as he took Douglas' place at the microphone.

"Me, too! I quit — hereby, forthwith, and all that other stuff!" He looked over to the remaining five members, who stood regarding him uncertainly, and flashed them a thumbs-up. Still they held back. He beckoned encouragingly.

Finally, Gerald ran up to the microphone. "I — I resign from the Grand Knights!"

Dave was hot on his heels. "I resign, too!"

Ric was next. "I'm out!" Followed by Yolanda, who announced, "I'm blowin' this popsicle stand!"

Anita was in crisis. She stood before the microphone, eyes wide, brow furrowed as though her brain were working triple-speed behind it. "I — "

She won't make it, Commando thought. The urge to be popular and important was too strong.

"I — quit . . . maybe . . . probably . . . No, I definitely quit!" She looked pleased. " 'Bye."

Once again, Douglas leaned in to the microphone.

"You may now call the roll." With all the pomp of an English butler, he shouldered his book bag and led a ceremonial procession off the stage and out of the gym. The six ex-Grand Knights followed, heads high, each step a thing of majesty.

The Richardsons were out on the stage, clapping and cheering themselves hoarse.

Mr. Silverman stared at them. "Martin — Julia — cut that out!"

But the couple celebrated on. "We're associate members!" Martin shouted back.

"I don't get it," complained Beverly in the front row. "What just happened?"

"I'll tell you what just happened!" laughed Carol. "Fairchild got you again! He got all of us! And we deserved it!"

Kahlil stepped forward. "Let's see how smart he is with his teeth knocked down his throat!"

Waldo grabbed him by the scruff of the neck and sat him down forcibly on the gym floor. "Will you shut up!?" And he called after the departing figures, "Way to go, Commando!"

As they stepped out onto the pavement of the playground, Commando nudged Douglas. "Hey, Doug, where are we going?"

"I told my parents I needed a ride home today." As if on cue, the long silver-gray limousine whispered around the corner of the parking lot.

Students poured out of the school, swarming in the playground, squinting in the late afternoon sunlight. An incredible sight met their eyes. A uniformed chauffeur held the door of the limo open and helped the seven members of the Special Discussion group inside. Eight hundred pairs of eyes watched transfixed as the driver closed his VIP's in the back, climbed in behind the wheel, and drove off.

The long silence that followed was broken by Beverly Busby. "Good riddance! Now let's go back inside so we can finish our meeting!"

The response to this was a chorus of jeers, snorts, and "forget its." Then the crowd dispersed, and everyone started for home.

"Where's everybody going?" Beverly demanded. "We're not finished yet! What's going on here?"

Carol put a sympathetic arm around her shoulders and led her away. "I'll explain it to you on the bus."

16

Disarming the Ultimate Stink Bomb

In the limo, the celebration was deafening.

"I can't believe it!" chortled Yolanda. "We *dissed* those guys! We *dissed* the whole school!"

Douglas was rummaging around the car's mini-bar, pouring ginger ale into champagne glasses.

"Do you realize," crowed Commando, "that everybody is now on the Twinkie Squad *except us?*"

"That's right!" exclaimed Gerald. "They called *us* Twinkies, and then *they* joined up!"

Douglas distributed the ginger ale. "A toast," he said, raising his glass.

"To who?" asked Dave.

"To *us*, man!" chortled Commando. "For years, everybody dumped on the Twinkies; today the Twinkies dumped on everybody!"

The limo tooled up streets, whispered around corners, and purred down avenues. Through the smoked glass of the windows, the nation's capital passed by, the majestic white buildings and monuments. The seven passengers, Grand Knights no more, but not Twinkies, either, sipped out of their crystal goblets, and gloried in the fact that they were now just — people.

Commando took a big gulp. "I guess we're still on the Twinkie Squad — like, we still have to go every day." He shrugged. "It could be worse. I like hanging out with you guys."

"You're my best friends," put in Gerald, and there was agreement all around.

"I think we should go together to see a movie," said Yolanda.

Commando groaned. "I've got a better idea. Actually, it's a *worse* idea. But we have to do it. Get the car turned around, Doug. We've got to get that squid out of the ceiling before the ratcatcher's men tear the whole school down."

Douglas reached into his book bag and pulled out a small saw. "I *was* going to do that myself. It's kind of you to offer your assistance."

"This is great!" exclaimed Gerald.

Commando stared at him. "Why?"

" 'Cause we're doing stuff! Stuff that only we can do!"

"I'll do the sawing," said Ric.

"I'll hold the chair for you," put in Anita.

"I'll stand guard!" Dave enthused.

The limo pulled up to the curb, and the Special Discussion Group thundered into the school, leaping up and punching the air in high spirits.

Douglas and Commando brought up the rear, walking at a normal pace. Commando was regarding his friend with a new respect. "You know, Doug, you're a great man — in your own way, every bit as great as your dad."

"Why?"

"Look at the Twinkie Squad — they're human! Gerald used to be afraid of his own shadow! Look how confident he is now. Dave's turned into a person, Ric's calming down a little — even Yolanda has a life that isn't based on some movie! And Anita — she has opinions! She says stuff that doesn't come from other people's mouths! Do you realize what you've done for these people?"

Douglas looked disappointed. "I thought you meant that my history of Pefkakia was destined to become a classic."

"This is way better!" Commando insisted. "The Richardsons went to college forever to get piles of counseling degrees. And in a million years they could never have done a thing with those Twinkies! But along comes you, and a couple of months later, everybody's cured!"

Douglas shrugged. "All I've ever done is try to proceed with Pefkakian dignity against bizarre and sometimes impossible odds."

Commando laughed. "You're either the smartest idiot, or the dumbest genius in the world!"

David Rivera was seated on a small chair outside Mr. Silverman's broom closet when Anton Fairchild wandered down the hall, looking for the location of his meeting with the principal. The ambassador recognized the other man and sighed with relief.

"Ah, thank goodness it's you. What's happened to this place? It smells like there's a dead body in here somewhere!"

The two men shook hands.

"The boys mentioned something about a smell," said Mr. Rivera, "but nobody said it was bad enough to drive the principal into a closet." He looked curious. "You think we're here about the same thing?"

"It seems like a good bet," nodded the ambassador.

At that moment, Mr. Silverman exploded out the door of *357–Storage*, arm outstretched. "Ambassador Fairchild!" he blurted out. "I had no idea *you* were coming! We were expecting your wife."

The ambassador shook the principal's hand gravely. "I, too, am related to Douglas," he admitted. "I believe you know Mr. Rivera?"

The principal escorted them inside, and the three sat down in the cramped quarters. "I apologize for the short notice, gentlemen, but I think you'll both agree that this is very, very serious." Mr. Silverman produced the Surgeon General's letter and laid it on the desk in front of the two fathers.

Holding wet paper towels tightly over their noses, the seven former Grand Knights snuck into the now-off-limits home ec room.

"Oh, man!" moaned Commando. "You ought to be shot for this, Doug!"

Douglas gurgled behind his towel. "If this school was run with a little more *glasnost*, I wouldn't have had to hide our lunch in the first place."

Gerald was gasping. "This is worse than foot powder day!"

Dave shook his head. "How could even squid smell this bad?"

"The mango, banana, and garlic probably made

things a little more pungent," Douglas confessed. He surveyed the ceiling. "It's right there."

"Are you positive?" asked Commando. "We're busting public property here. We don't want to make two holes."

Ric began sawing slowly.

Ambassador Fairchild was pale as a ghost. "He said it was for a project!" he managed weakly. "He misused the signature of the Surgeon General! That's probably a felony!"

Mr. Rivera was still staring at the letter. "I don't get it. What's this supposed to be about?"

"About the time Armando beat up Douglas in the schoolyard," replied the principal.

"But they're best friends!" cried David Rivera in amazement.

"Here's what happened," the principal explained. "There was a commotion in the schoolyard, and when I got there, Douglas had a bloody nose, and Armando was standing over him. Two days later, they tried to feed me a phony story about how Douglas was writing in his yellow binder and wouldn't put it down to catch a basketball. Did you ever hear anything so ridiculous?"

"Oh, boy." The ambassador's head was in his hands. When he looked up, his eyes were twin steel knives that sliced right through the principal. "You've punished an innocent boy!"

Mr. Silverman shook his head. "Sir, it's very common for a bully to intimidate his victims so that they're afraid to inform against him."

"Yes, yes, I understand that," said Mr. Fairchild. "Except for one thing: Douglas wouldn't put down that binder if a cruise missile was coming at his face, let alone a basketball!"

The principal turned deathly pale.

Mr. Rivera's mouth hardened into a thin line. "My son is not a bully. The people he fights with are bullies, picking on younger kids. If you were really on top of what's going on at your school, you'd know that!"

Mr. Silverman was silent for a long time. When he finally spoke, his voice was low and choked. "What I did here goes against everything I've ever believed in. How could I have been so blind?"

"It's rather obvious," said Ambassador Fairchild coldly. "You ignored the circumstances, and assumed that the ambassador's son was blameless, and the boy with the earring was at fault."

Mr. Silverman turned to David Rivera. "Of course Armando will be reinstated to the basketball team, and this incident will be erased from his record."

"And one more thing," added Commando's father. "You're going to tell him you were wrong, and you're sorry."

The principal flushed. "Of course you're right, sir. I owe him that."

The permanent ceiling installation was strong. Even with Ric, then Commando, then Douglas sawing at top speed, it took a good ten minutes to make the hole. The instant the opening was complete, the paralyzing stench tripled in intensity.

Ric hugged his towel closer to his nose. "We're not going to make it! I'm going to pass out!"

"We must be close," gagged Douglas. "It's quite strong."

"Quite strong!?" wailed Commando. "The grass is dying outside! The Washington Monument's wilting! The Potomac's turning to blood!"

Douglas reached both long arms into the hole and felt around. "Jackpot!" He drew out a greasy, dripping, slimy paper bag. The smell was more horrible than anyone had dreamed possible. Their eyes began to water, their noses to burn.

Anita burst into tears. "I'm sorry!" she blubbered. "I got sprayed by a skunk once, and it was *nothing* compared to this!"

Gerald ran to the paper towel dispenser and emptied it. He helped Douglas wrap the monstrosity completely in an inch and a half of paper. The sludge of decaying garlic squid with mango and banana soaked right through. The smell did not abate.

"You expected Willy and Milly to *eat this*?" cried Dave in outrage. "I should report you to the ASPCA!"

"Where can we throw it out?" Douglas mused with a juicy snort. His postnasal drip was back.

"It'll stink up the world!" Commando gasped. "Come on! Let's take it out in the yard and bury it!"

Holding the lethal package out in front of him like a waiter delivering a gourmet dinner on a silver tray, Douglas started for the door. Yolanda grabbed a handful of teaspoons to serve as digging equipment.

"Are you crazy?" roared Commando. "It'll take a month to dig with those!"

"I once saw a movie where a guy struck oil with a pickle fork!" Yolanda retorted smugly.

"Just keep moving!" Ric begged. "I'm dying!"

Douglas led the way through the empty hall, up the stairs, and out into the schoolyard. They stumbled across the concrete to the first unpaved area, a sickly flower bed planted around a memorial plaque to Thaddeus G. Little. There they all began digging frantically with their teaspoons.

"Make it deep," Douglas advised.

"What if the worms union complains?" muttered Commando and kept on digging. One thought occupied his mind — the sooner that squid was underground, the sooner they could all breathe again. His arm worked like a machine, the spoon just a blur.

He felt a tap on his shoulder, but did not break his rhythm. Another tap, harder this time.

"Bug off, Doug! I'm trying to get this stupid thing buried!"

A throat cleared — definitely not a middle-schooler's. Commando lifted his head. He saw the shoes first, shiny black leather, size twelve. His eyes traveled up — blue pants, blue jacket, badge. A District of Columbia police officer stood over the flower bed, one hand on his nightstick, the other holding Douglas firmly by the arm. The rest of the group cowered there, looking guilty.

"This fighting thing is clear out of left field for me," Ambassador Fairchild was saying. "I thought this was about Douglas' midterm. The boy isn't doing his work. He needs help. And he's not getting it, because you assume that *my* son couldn't possibly have problems."

Mr. Silverman was still shaken from the realization that he had wronged Commando. "Well," he began uncertainly, "it's just that Douglas is such an overpowering boy — "

"Tell me about it," said the ambassador ironically.

"He's well spoken and intelligent," the principal continued. "I guess we all thought his poor grades were due to lack of effort."

"My wife and I always thought so, too," said the ambassador. He shrugged helplessly. "But maybe the time has come to consider the possibility that Douglas — well" — he raised an eyebrow — "isn't as bright as we think he is."

"You're way off-base," put in Mr. Rivera sharply. "I don't know what kind of student he is, but I find him creative, and incredibly loyal. He's a great kid."

The ambassador turned to Mr. Rivera gratefully. "That's the first nice thing anybody's said about Douglas since 'It's a boy.' And they said that in Pef-kakian." He smiled. "You ought to be very proud of Commando. He's a fine young man. I couldn't have asked for a better friend for Douglas."

At that moment, the policeman barged in, herding his captives. "I caught these characters outside burying a big stink." He held up the dripping mass of squid and paper towel, and the three man recoiled from the stench. "Who's in charge of the Magnificent Seven?"

"I am," admitted Mr. Rivera, hand clamped over his nose, eyes on Commando.

"I am," confessed the ambassador, gawking at Douglas from behind the lapel of his silk suit.

"I am," echoed Mr. Silverman, glaring at the ooz-ing bundle of pure odor that had held his school hostage for over a month.

Commando lay on his bed, staring at the ceiling. His father had barely said two words to him since they'd met unceremoniously in Mr. Silverman's broom closet. All the way home, all through dinner, there had been no conversation. He didn't mind being in trouble, but the silent treatment from David Rivera was brutal torture.

He got up and began to pace the small room. His eyes darted to the unfinished letter to his mother on the desk. It read: *Dear Mom, How are you? I am fine. Everything's great here.* Yeah, right. David Rivera was so mad that maybe nothing would be the same between them ever again.

There was a knock at the door, and Mr. Rivera entered, his face grim. "Comm, I want to tell you something, and I want to be sure that you understand every word, because this is very important."

Commando nodded, steeling himself. Here it came. *You lied about the basketball team, you hid your midterm, you were caught with a health hazard, you were arrested! I'm throwing you out into the street! You're no son of mine!*

What Mr. Rivera actually said was, "I passed the test."

Commando's heart leaped. "You *what*? You're a CPA? Really?"

Mr. Rivera nodded.

"All right, Dad!" Commando threw himself at his father, grabbing him around the waist, and toppling them both to the floor. "Rivera, CPA! It's got a nice ring to it!"

"Hey, listen, Comm," said Mr. Rivera, getting up on one knee. "Don't ever do this again, okay? You can tell me *anything*. I'd never believe you'd hit a guy for no reason."

"I couldn't get you all upset when you had to study," explained Commando.

"You can get me upset any time at all! Besides" —
his eyes gleamed — "I'm never going to have to
study again as long as I live! I have taken my *last*
exam!"

"Don't rub it in," grinned Commando. "I've got
ten years of them ahead of me." He punched his
father lightly in the stomach. "Man, I thought you
were going to kill me!"

"For what? You're not a bully, you only lied a little
to keep the pressure off me, you even tried to help
Doug get rid of the squid! All in all, Comm, when
they were handing out sons, I did" — he thought it
over, and shrugged — "fair to not bad."

It was stupid, Commando thought, to get so
blurry-eyed over being called "not bad." So he
reached out and put his father in a headlock.

"Come on, CPA! Fair to *good!* Fair to *good!*"

Mr. Rivera lifted him bodily and tossed him onto
his bed. "Stay there, and try not to get arrested
again!" he laughed. "I've got to go phone everybody
in the world, and gloat!" And he ran out in the direction of the telephone.

Commando lay back on his pillow and sighed with
contentment. What a day! It was amazing to think
that, after all those twists of fate, the roller coaster
had dropped him off on pretty high ground. Things
had worked out well for everyone — except Doug.

Poor Doug. Doug *was* responsible for the smell
in the school, and Doug *did* spearhead the Grand
Knights, and Doug *had* achieved a report card
worthy of a below-average orangutan. He was in big
trouble! Of course, he would just pull out the old
Pefkakian argument — "For an American student,
this would be terrible, but for a Pefkakian . . ."

Or would he? Maybe Mr. and Mrs. Fairchild didn't buy the Pefkakia stuff. Come to think of it, Commando wasn't so sure he bought it himself.

He leaned over to the shelf that held his *World Book Encyclopedia* and reached for the volume marked *P*.

17

Frolicking Amidst the Bullrushes

The weekend did much to clear out the smell in the school now that the squid was gone. Mr. Silverman remained in *357–Storage*, and the home ec room would be off-limits for several weeks, but things were on their way back to normal.

Commando found Douglas cleaning out his locker before first period Monday morning. "Hey, Doug. Rough weekend?"

Douglas dropped his gym clothes into a large Saks' shopping bag. "It wasn't great," he admitted.

"I called all day yesterday," said Commando. "You didn't get back to me."

Douglas didn't answer. Then he said, "I have to go to another school."

"What? Why?" At first, Commando was outraged. But after a moment's thought, he knew why. Douglas wasn't doing any work at Thaddeus G. Little. He sat through classes writing in his binder. Commando should have known that it couldn't last forever.

"It's a special school for people who have problems concentrating," Douglas said quietly. "I explained that the real problem was my Pefkakian mind set, but nobody agreed."

Commando nodded. "My dad passed his test," he said after a moment.

Douglas' face lit up. "That's great. Tell him congratulations from me." He returned to the business of emptying his locker into the bag. His next sentence was almost a whisper. "I don't want to go to that new school."

The bell rang, and the hallways cleared as the students hurried to class. Commando made no move to follow. He shifted his weight uncomfortably. "Hey, Doug, just because you'll be going to a different school doesn't mean we can't hang out together. You know — evenings, weekends, booby-trapping my dad — but not *your* dad — "

"Burying squid," Douglas added.

Commando grinned. "Do you realize that when the cop caught us, he thought we had somebody's *head* in that bag?"

Douglas almost smiled. But as he returned to the business of packing his things, it was obvious that he was really down.

"Listen, Doug," Commando began carefully, "I looked up Pefkakia in the encyclopedia last night."

No response from Douglas.

Commando forged on. "There *is* no Pefkakia anymore. It was only a country for six months before Saudi Arabia swallowed it up. And even then, they never had a U.S. embassy. No offense, Doug, but I don't see how you could have been born there."

Douglas' eyes gleamed. "My parents were stationed in New Delhi. They were flying home for my sister's graduation, and my mother went into labor on the plane. They landed at the nearest airport — Pefkakia City — and I was born in the first-aid station behind the baggage claim."

Commando was fascinated. "How long did you live there?"

"Twelve hours. After that we flew straight to Washington." He lowered his eyes. "I never made it to any bullrushes."

"You really *are* a Pefkakian!" Commando exclaimed. "Sorry I doubted you, man."

Douglas reached into his book bag and pulled out his yellow binder. "Since you're the only one who understands my background, I've decided to let you read my history of Pefkakia."

Commando was deeply honored. "You mean it?"

Douglas held out the binder. "Please."

Commando accepted it and opened to Page One. It read:

> *Blah blah blah blah blah blah blah blah*
> *Blah blah blah blah blah blah blah blah*
> *Blah blah blah blah blah blah blah blah*

Stunned, he flipped ahead. All the pages were the same. Reams of looseleaf were jammed with *blahs*. *Blah* inserts were written in the margins. *Blahs* were crossed out, and replaced with other *blahs*. Seventy-two numbered pages (in Roman numerals) held thousands of that single word — *blah*.

Commando pictured Douglas in class, at lunch,

on the bus, in Special Discussion Group, *slaving* over the yellow binder! This is what he was writing? Blah? This is why he had no time to do his homework and get better grades? Blah?

He felt like strangling Douglas. It was his own fault that he was getting sent to a special school! While he was writing this — this *garbage*, he could have been doing his work!

And in a flash, Commando understood. Here was Doug, youngest of a family of heavy-duty winners — an ambassador, a super-hostess, a congressman, and a brilliant doctor. How could he compete? He couldn't. The Pefkakia thing had made him not better, but *different*. It had kept him out of the race.

Head spinning, Commando tore his eyes from the binder. Douglas was regarding him intently, waiting for some comment.

"It's — it's not that good," he managed.

Douglas nodded.

"I've seen worse," Commando added quickly.

"Thank you."

The two stood there for what seemed like a long time, staring at the binder in Douglas' hands.

"What now?" Commando said finally.

"I was thinking of having it serialized in a magazine prior to publication," Douglas replied.

Now it was Commando's turn to nod.

"Or I could just burn it," Douglas finished.

"I'll help," Commando decided.

The two snuck out of the school building to the back alley where the garbage cans were kept. Commando found an empty metal barrel, and Douglas dropped his yellow binder inside. It lay in the bottom, open to page XLIV.

Douglas struck a match and stood there, holding it uncertainly.

"What about all that stuff?" Commando prodded. "You know — Grand Knights, medieval biathlon, trikas, the Karpoozi river — ?"

The match was burning down to Douglas' fingers. "I may have exaggerated a little."

"A *little*?"

"I made it up — all except for Ano Pefki. He's real." He released the match. The pages caught immediately and were consumed before their eyes. The light from the flames played across their faces. They watched, transfixed, as endless rows of *blahs* turned brown, then black, then disappeared. The *History of Pefkakia* was no more.

It was a long time before Douglas raised his gaze from the trash barrel. Commando watched him, wondering what he would say now that his life's work was gone.

Douglas cast him a penetrating look. "Did your encyclopedia happen to mention that the immortal Ano Pefki was a bus driver?"

Commando looked up at him, an enormous grin splitting his face. "I wasn't going to say anything if you didn't. Hey, Doug, I've got to get to class. Silverman likes me right now, but I'm not going to push my luck."

"I'll stay here a while," said Douglas, "to keep an eye on the fire."

"Call you tonight," said Commando and ran off.

But there was no fire left to watch. Douglas turned away from the ashes and stopped in surprise. His father's silver-gray limousine was parked at the curb.

The driver was half an hour early. Sighing, he trudged towards the car. He stopped again. There was Anton Fairchild walking across the schoolyard, struggling with a giant flowerpot.

"Dad?"

"Hi, Douglas," beamed the ambassador. He put down the pot and climbed in among the tall shoots of grassy brown plant. "Guess what I'm doing?"

Douglas stared. "Are you okay?"

"I'll give you a hint," called Mr. Fairchild. He began to run in place in the pot, kicking dirt in all directions.

"Dad, stop that!" Douglas was horrified. "What if the press sees you?"

"I'm *frolicking amidst the bullrushes!*" roared the ambassador. "And don't think it's easy to find a Washington florist who has bullrushes!"

Douglas gawked. Yes, those were real bullrushes, and that was real frolicking. One question remained: "Why are you doing this?"

"I called the new school and told them forget it."

"Yeah?" Even staid and impassive Douglas could not keep the huge grin from his face. "What made you change your mind?"

The ambassador grinned back. "A few of the experts came by my office this morning. They seem to think this place can't do without you."

The back door of the limo opened and out poured Gerald, Dave, Anita, Yolanda, and Ric, all clapping and cheering.

Commando's upper body appeared at a first-floor classroom window. He whistled and waved until a foghorn voice bellowed, *"Armando!"* and he disappeared in a flash.

The ambassador turned serious. "You're going to do better, right, Douglas? You're not going to make monkeys out of the experts and me?"

"You have my word as a Pef — I promise, Dad!"

His father held out both hands. "Hop in. I bought enough bullrushes for two."

About the Author

Gordon Korman has written over fifteen books for children and young adults, including three ALA Best Books for Young Adults, *Son of Interflux*, *A Semester in the Life of a Garbage Bag*, and *Losing Joe's Place*. When he was twelve, he wrote his first book, *This Can't Be Happening at Macdonald Hall*, about the adventures of two friends, Bruno and Boots. He published five other books by the time he was graduated from high school, and has written five other books about Bruno and Boots, most recently *Macdonald Hall Goes Hollywood*.

A native of Ontario, Canada, and a graduate of New York University's School of Dramatic Writing, Korman divides his time between Toronto and New York City and writes full time.